COMMUNICATION
RECONCILIATION

COMMUNICATION RECONCILIATION

Challenges Facing the 21st Century

Edited by
Philip Lee

WCC Publications, Geneva
World Association for Christian Communication, London

© 2001 World Association for Christian Communication
357 Kennington Lane
London SE11 5QY, UK

Cover design: Rob Lucas

Published by WCC Publications
World Council of Churches
150 route de Ferney, P.O. Box 2100
1211 Geneva 2, Switzerland
Website: http://www.wcc-coe.org

ISBN 2-8254-1341-0

Printed in Switzerland

Contents

Introduction
Breaking the Chains of Inhumanity: Stories on the Way to Reconciliation

CARLOS A. VALLE

How do we tear down the barriers that deprive people of communication? How do we communicate the promise of a new humanity to those people who have been denied everything? Is there any way of changing this situation? Is reconciliation, for example, a realistic, adequate, viable way of breaking the chains of inhumanity that bind both those who suffer as well as those who perpetuate suffering?

Humanity has been strengthened, especially so over the last hundred years. That progress has been achieved is self-evident. For example, most, if not all, of the major technological developments in the field of communications – radio, television, satellites and computers – emerged during the modern era. It was assumed that all this progress was going to benefit humankind. The global situation today, however, presents a different story. Our world has been repeatedly broken by wars, the degradation of nature, economic exploitation and poverty. Stories from East Timor, Myanmar, Indonesia, Rwanda, Sierra Leone, Angola, the Middle East and many other places remind us of the suffering of many people – of starving children, people uprooted from their countries and homes, innocent victims of war and ethnic conflicts.

These and other stories also remind us that we live in a globalized world in which money and power are becoming more important than people – slave labour has become the basis for profitable production, the poor have become disposable and the destruction of the earth is an ongoing process. In this context, communication continues to play a dominant role in accelerating the evolution of globalization. These processes linked to globalization have been strengthened by technological developments, the concentration of media-power in the hands of a few people and corporations, the expansion of satellite-based television broadcasting and the creation of information superhighways. They are providing information, expressing values and impinging forcefully on the configuration of human relationships.

Quite often, we are overwhelmed by these developments and are unable to take advantage of the opportunities they offer. New communication technologies are marvellous tools, gifts from God. But as in the case of every gift, we need to know how to use them. The dazzling possibilities offered by new technologies in no way guarantee access to, or the acquisition of, quality knowledge. We cannot ignore the fact that these new technologies will facilitate the broadening of horizons and the extension of contacts, thus leading to new ways of encountering and living globally and locally.

Unfortunately, the structures of modern communication, weighed down by monolithic patterns of ownership and control, are encouraging the trivial, elitist and authoritarian at the expense of the substantive. Today we are aware that democracy means much more than a person's right to say or to know. In a village context, every word spoken finds an echo in the community. The city has turned this experience into an illusion. The city has its own rules. One has access to community provided one has access to the media. As history has repeatedly demonstrated, however, when people are denied access to the media, they still find ways to communicate.

The purpose of this book is to explore a variety of perspectives on the role played by communication in the search for reconciliation. The contributions come from people located in different countries and focus on very concrete, particular situations. These chapters do not pretend to account for or cover all perspectives related to the theme. Rather, they are examples of some ways in which the theme can be explored. If there is a thread that runs through these different accounts, it is the affirmation that reconciliation is a process that can start only when the "other" is accepted as one's neighbour. For such an acceptance, it is necessary to review one's own history together with that of the other, to learn and to listen to the other, to acknowledge the history of the other as a common history, to confess jointly for past wrongs, enabling the "enemy" to be recognized as human and locating mutuality at the heart of building community.

What do the chapters point towards? Wesley Ariarajah affirms that what is required is a "culture of dialogue". Reconciliation is predicated on prior acknowledgment of the validity of the many varieties of cultures and historical experiences in our multicultural and multireligious world. At least four elements are critical to this process. First, the understanding of communication as relationship: "The truth of the message depends on who carries it and why." Second, the role played by language: "Words have their own history of meaning." Language consists of a number of different sounds, but these sounds convey meanings to those who speak the same language. Language is a source of identity, affections and personal growth. Third, the enemy of communication is prejudice, defined as "judgment made without actual knowledge, which one has come to believe to be true".

Finally, on the role played by religion, Ariarajah provides examples from the increasing tension between Hindu and Christian communities in India. He is convinced that "many conflicts arise from the fact that the stories do not connect". The politicization of such conflicts points to the fact that it is impossible to analyze religious conflicts without paying adequate attention to the relationships between politics and culture.

Analyzing the situation in the USA, William F. Fore is convinced that it is necessary to consider the nature of alienation in any examination of reconciliation. He offers twelve propositions on democracy. He states that one reason for the USA's democratic deficit is the role played by "the communication industry... in creating alienation and defeating the democratic process".

Fore criticizes media responsibility and rues the fact that "every organized activity has become commodified" and that the USA is becoming a home to "corporate people" who are not in the least "civic-minded". He implicates the communication industry in the suppression of democracy "through control of the political process". But this problem has wider global ramifications because in the context of a globalized world "new communication empires are global extensions of the capitalist system" and are "inherently anti-democratic and... deeply alienating".

There is little space for religion in this context. "America is not a 'Christian' nation", and the 21st century "will see a fight between religion and fantasy" and a "radical individualism". Problems that have to do with our globalized world need to be considered by Christians in terms of "religious issues". The churches ought to be involved in educating their members about their rights and responsibilities as citizens and mobilizing them to take concrete action – for instance, a political campaign geared to bringing about the financial reform of media industries.

Dafne Sabanes Plou explores the relationship between truth and reconciliation. She recalls the tragic years of dictatorship in Argentina and the manner in which silence and terror were imposed by means of persecution, torture and murder. She acknowledges the efforts made by many people, especially women, who challenged the oppressive regime with their courage and determination. When people are silenced, even symbols speak. The headscarves that the mothers and grandmothers of the Plaza de Mayo wore with the names of the disappeared "became symbols of a denunciation that penetrated looks and minds". Their message "was stronger and more persuasive than all the propaganda broadcast by radio and television".

The courage of people marching in peace, despite the prohibition imposed by the military regime, "generated the hoped-for communication". After all the long years of dictatorship "people had to reconcile themselves to the truth". For many this came about through a confession of their self-imposed blindness to the truth. To rescue and to preserve memory is at times a painful experience, but it is also purifying because "living with the truth makes people and nations honourable and free".

Tissa Balasuriya offers a perspective on communication ethics based on a "pluralist worldview" through engagement with a complex world – a context that is characterized by profit as the main motivation "rather than truth, justice and right relationships among peoples". For Balasuriya, "what exists today is a white, racist world order of nation-states built during the past five centuries by the West, mainly by force". He believes that we need to move from "plural worldviews" to a "pluralist worldview", which assumes that humankind is one family. In this pluralist worldview "opportunities must be provided for differing perspectives to be expressed, especially for the poor and oppressed".

The aim of communication should be "the human common good". Today, the media are profit driven, conditioning citizens to become passive consumers, denying them the opportunities to deal with deeper realities. This negative role has created a culture based on selfishness and self-gratification. For Balasuriya, "A basic factor surrounding the entire issue of communications is the prevailing world apartheid," created, among others, by Western colonial invasions, consolidation of territorial frontiers, and unjust immigration laws that have denied many people a share of the world's wealth and resources. These injustices remind us that what is required is "a global communications ethic" supportive of truth, memory and justice.

In this multiethnic and multiracial world the question of who we are needs to be addressed. Identity "is created in social interaction", but "it can be changed, destroyed and reconstructed", affirms Epp Lauk from her own experiences in Estonia. There are three basic elements of any national identity: language, cultural traditions and history. They played and are still playing a significant role in rebuilding Estonia after the collapse of the Soviet Union. For the Estonian people "the mother tongue had always been... a symbol of human dignity", but one that was deeply affected by political and economic events. As in many other parts of the world, however, people resisted using "metaphoric language", writing and reading "between the lines". After the Soviet collapse it was necessary to work towards a new identity. For Lauk, economic development "has helped to stabilize interethnic relationships", preventing "outbursts of violence and conflict". At the same time, the liberalized economy of the newly globalized environment placed new challenges in the path of reconciliation.

Where can the wisdom to face these new realities be found? Bernie Harder and Marlene Cuthbert believe that there is a lot to be learned from the First Nations peoples of Canada. "The spirit of community" is central to their worldviews. "Community is based on spirit – the Creator – and is fundamentally related to the land." Colonialism led to the disintegration of community, and harmony can be achieved only when the wounds are healed. We learn of the struggle of Native persons for "liberation, survival, and beyond to affirmation". "The Creator gave us our spiritual beliefs, our languages, our culture, and a place on Mother Earth who provided us with all our needs."

But how can community be regained? When the "purpose is healing not punishment". "Peace-making is more conciliation than it is mediation. It is relationship-centred, not agreement-centred" (Diane LeResche). The churches in Canada are involved in what they have admitted is "a long and painful journey" for their own healing and in terms of their relationships with the people belonging to the First Nations. The authors affirm that reconciliation begins when there is an acknowledgment that "we can be human only in community".

Jahda Abou Khalil and Nawaf Kabbara are committed to "integration" and believe that reconciliation begins when people begin to respect people with disabilities. Their marginalization from society is not caused by their own physical and mental situation but is "the product of the insensitivity of society to the needs of these people, in terms of both social attitudes and failure to provide physical accessibility. The question of disability became one of human rights and tolerance."

Khalil and Kabbara note that disability as an issue of human rights has yet to find a place on the agenda of organizations like the UN. They "have not yet started to tackle the issue and do not know how to deal with it". Both are convinced that "only through empowering people with disabilities and building disability as a social identity can the cause of disability be addressed as a political and human rights issue".

For V. Geetha an ideology of exclusion is a barrier to reconciliation. "Today's gestures of public remorse seek to acquire for themselves the poignancy that is inherent to penitential acts without actually giving it material form and coherence." At the same time, "those who are the objects of remorse and reconciliation have neither the political energy and resources nor the authority to enforce penitence". Her story from India, based on the case of untouchability, illustrates the efforts to expand "the limits to a politics of reconciliation". She argues that Mahatma Gandhi "brought to politics a sense of moral seriousness". To him "untouchability was morally wrong". He believed that by serving people, one took part in politics. Both the possibilities and limits of his ethics of reconciliation were demonstrated through Gandhian praxis.

In contrast, Gandhi's critic Dr Ambedkar insisted that a radically different relationship between politics and ethics was needed to tackle untouchability. He believed that untouchability was sustained by an "economics that is pitiless and a civics that is cynical" and that it was "a system of uncontrolled economic exploitation". Ambedkar believed that Hinduism was not the answer, for it was incapable of accepting untouchables as equal citizens. His personal response was conversion to Buddhism because it offered radical civic possibilities. For Ambedkar, "Buddhism appeared an appropriate choice because it was a religion that centred on human beings and not God."

The richness of the experiences outlined in this book challenges us to broaden our understanding of reconciliation, which is at the heart of the Christian message. The good news embodies genuine reconciliation. We are in need of communication that humanizes; that speaks of persons, not numbers; that speaks of peoples' needs, their suffering and their dreams. When communication acquires such a human face, it will become a force for reconciliation.

Creating a "Culture of Dialogue" in a Multicultural and Pluralist Society

S. WESLEY ARIARAJAH

My deepest awareness of the problems of communication in pluralist societies came home to me at a meeting in my own country, Sri Lanka. A group of us from the majority Sinhalese community and the minority Tamil community had met to discuss the violent and senseless conflict that has plagued the island for decades. We were all well-meaning and reasonable persons committed to peace and harmony. All of us, at least in our own assessment of ourselves, were well informed about the history and the socio-political developments in the country that had brought about the conflict.

As the meeting proceeded, I became aware that there were in fact not one but two conversations in process, that we had different starting points, different experiences, different perceptions, and different stakes in the issues. Yes, we were indeed in conversation, but we were not in communication with each other! It was a humbling experience for me to realize that despite the pretences and protestations to the contrary, all of us had too much "baggage" of our own and too little awareness of the experience of the other to be able to communicate meaningfully with one another.

The time we live in has been aptly characterized as the Information Age. The methods and speed of communication have advanced by leaps and bounds. The amount of information available, the speed with which people can be in touch with each other and the resources available to bring parties in conflict into contact have all increased beyond even the wildest imagination of our parents. And yet we have begun also this third millennium with numerous conflicts and confrontations, tensions and outright wars. In despair we join the cry: Where is the knowledge we have lost in the information explosion? Where is all the wisdom we have lost with the piling up of our knowledge?

Difficulty encountered in the conversation between the two language groups in Sri Lanka is multiplied many times when the conversation is between persons drawn from radically different cultures and religious traditions. It is made worse when corporate historical experiences have shaped the collective memories of the peoples in conversation. The intractable difficulties in seeking a negotiated peace and reconciliation in the Israeli-Palestinian conflict, for example, as one is painfully aware, have little to do with finding a formula or a compromise but with the corporate historical consciousness that each community brings into the conversation. The mutual distrust is so strong that there is mutual suspicion even about the real intentions of entering into the conversation. The scars of previous wars remain, the wounds having been healed only on the surface.

The conflict over Kosovo, the breaking up of the former Yugoslavia, and the ruthless violence perpetuated on each other by persons who had until then been neighbours and friends baffles those who have not been part of the historical memories that have shaped the communities in the Balkans.

In a similar manner, conversations between Western Christians and Arab Muslims on such issues as human rights, rights of women, relationship between religion and state often run on parallel lines, with little or no chance of a meeting of minds. The African expressions of tribal loyalties and the capacity of the Japanese to cling to tradition in the context of massive technological advances have amazed outsiders who have attempted to negotiate either political settlements or business deals with persons and groups from these cultures.

The Western preoccupation with freedom of the individual and with one particular form of organizing economic life, primarily as a reaction to its own history in the Middle Ages, is little understood in some other cultures. Its insistence on the separation between religion and state is shaped by the experience of liberation and freedom that came with the dawn of the era of Enlightenment in Europe and is not necessarily the experience of those other cultures.

In other words, our cultures, group loyalties, historical experiences and current existential necessities shape all of us. Meetings between peoples and communities do not take place in a vacuum. All our conversations are coloured by who we are and what we carry with us. In a pluralistic world all attempts to communicate or to bring about reconciliation that ignore these realities can have only limited success.

Communication as relationships

In the celebrated Indian epic *Ramayana,* we encounter an interesting dimension of what is intended in communication. Ravana, the evil ruler of the island of Sri Lanka, has kidnapped Sita, the heroine. Rama, the hero of the epic, sends his monkey companion, Hanuman, across the sea to communicate the message of his plans to liberate her. In the fascinating account of the encounter between Sita and Hanuman, Sita is little concerned with the message until she is given proof of Hanuman's knowledge of her relationship with her husband and of her husband's relationship with Hanuman. The communication makes sense for Sita only in the context of established relationships. The truth of the message depends on who carries it and why.

In all cultures communication and relationships are inseparable. The relationships between husband and wife, parents and children, the leader and followers of a tribe and so forth demand constant communication between the parties. But this communication is not separate from what one would describe as their relationships. In this context languages developed as by-products of these relationships, to enhance and enrich them, rather than to create them. Originally, languages as tools of communication were internal to the communities that spoke them. They emerged to further enable and embellish relationships that already existed. They were to be neither learned nor used by those outside the community. Words, phrases and sayings therefore have special shades of meaning, connotations and histories that outsiders never understand. Languages are innate to peoples' being; it is difficult to separate a people's language from their culture, history and emotions.

The limitations of language in cross-cultural communication

Today some languages, especially English, have been used across many cultures in bringing about reconciliation and peace. Anyone who is involved in these efforts knows that the same English words have different shades of meaning in different cultures and can lead to misunderstanding. The words have their own history of meaning and undergo considerable changes in what they signify when they are embedded into different cultures.

People who translate scriptures, books or documents from one language to another would testify to the enormous difficulties that one encounters in communication across cultures. At times, the corresponding word in the language into which a foreign word is translated has a different shade of meaning. At other times, a word in English could be translated into four possible different local words, each carrying a different nuance of meaning. On other occasions the corresponding word or idea just does not exist in another culture.

One of the first attempts to translate the Bible from its original Hebrew and Greek texts into Tamil was made in Jaffna, the heartland of the Tamil-speaking people of Sri Lanka. Peter Percival, a great scholar and Methodist missionary to Sri Lanka, undertook the task of translation, recruiting the assistance of Arumuga Navalar, one of the celebrated Hindu Tamil scholars of that time. The effort to translate the New Testament, despite many minor problems, progressed rather well until they came to the word in the New Testament translated by the English word "hope".

Percival felt that the Tamil words they were coming up with did not capture the richness of the word "hope" but rather meant "faith", "trust" or "expectation". After much struggle to resolve the problem, Percival asked Navalar, in desperation, "What is the Hindu word you use to describe what you are sure will happen in the future, but for which you now have to wait with patience?"

Navalar was surprised. "How can one know what is going to happen in the future?" he asked. "And how can one be so sure about something yet to happen that one waits for it with patience?" For him the only phrase that would have translated that particular attitude into Tamil would be "wishful thinking".

It turned out that in fact Tamil has no word with the New Testament idea of hope as an assured thing one waits for, which was distinct from "faith", "trust", "expectation" and so forth. At the end of 1 Corinthians 13, Paul says, "Now abide faith, hope and love. But the greatest of these is love." The Tamil Bible had to use the Sanskritized Tamil word for faith *(visuvasam)* to translate "faith", and the actual Tamil word for faith *(nambikkai)* to translate "hope"! It was up to the preachers to help the second word, which in common parlance had exactly the same meaning as the first, gradually accrue the rich meaning of the New Testament concept of a "certain hope", "living hope" and so on.

Communication based on language thus has its own limitations. Furthermore, there has been a proliferation of words and symbols in our day. They have been so misused and abused in our cultures that they have gradually lost their power to evoke and inspire – or in other words, to communicate effectively. And yet we put so much trust in words and documents signed by dignitaries as vehicles to communicate and bring about reconciliation. In a world of plurality of cultures, traditions, religions and ways of life, communication needs to be understood in its deeper dimensions.

Dialogue as a mode of communication

In recent years the concept of dialogue has emerged as a key component in understanding communication in a multicultural and pluralistic society. Unfortunately, the word "dialogue" conjures up an image of two persons or two groups of persons sitting across a table engaging in serious conversations. Even though it includes such conversations, in reality the word has come to mean much more. Dialogue, it has been said, is a "way of life" in pluralistic societies. We also speak about a "spirit of dialogue", a "spirituality of dialogue" and a "culture of dialogue".

Dialogue is thus more than conversations. It concerns the way we relate to one another in multicultural and pluralistic societies and involves the disciplines that should inform and dictate our relationships. It seeks to bring out the pre-requisites for communication across barriers. It lays bare the pre-conditions often needed for communities to move beyond confrontation to a spirit of reconciliation. What, then, are some of the principles of dialogue as a means of communication?

Mutual respect. "He doesn't respect me; why should I listen to him?" We hear this statement all too often. Real communication between two groups of people is effective only when they have a basic respect for one another. Each community that wishes to speak, however, must earn the right to be heard. In all pluralistic situations such a right to be heard is earned by the respect given to the community one seeks to relate to. Earning such respect comes through one's willingness to accept the "otherness" of the others. That is, basic respect for plurality or of other ways of being, believing and acting is at the heart of the spirituality of dialogue.

In pluralistic situations communication that does not respect plurality is experienced as oppressive or "colonial". A "colonial mind" expects everyone to respect and embrace its own way of life as the only true way of life. In such "colonial" situations the will of the one is imposed on the other through the exercise of power, subtle or overt. Much work on reconciliation fails to take into account this important dimension of human relationship.

Listening and learning. Respect for otherness, however, cannot be generated for isolated situations but must be developed as a spirituality that marks one's attitude and approach to others. It is difficult, for example, for some from an urbanized Western culture to arrive in an African village and suddenly begin to like and respect everything that he or she sees. It is of course possible superficially to respect the reality into which one has come merely by not engaging in uninformed criticism of the new. But true respect and a critical appreciation of what one has come into contact with can happen only through a long process of listening and learning.

Any meaningful communication between the newcomer and the people of the village can happen only when the new person gains a reasonable knowledge of the structure and life of the community, the way relationships are exercised, the meaning and place of rites and rituals and so forth. Respect is thus nurtured through a process of listening and learning. It is such nurtured respect that leads to effective communication and empathetic solidarity between the community and the newcomer.

The example applies to the wider issues of communication between persons, communities and nations. Many of the communication difficulties in the conflict situations of the world also involve the lack of listening and learning. Often people from the outside arrive with what to them appears to be a perfect solution to the problem and are surprised by the "unwillingness" of the parties concerned to accept and implement it. Unfortunately, when attempts at negotiations are contrived or are imposed from the outside, negotiations become places to which people bring their own grievances and demands. In most such cases the rehearsing of the respective grievances and demands only helps to keep them apart rather than bringing them any closer.

An outsider indeed has an important role in mediating and enabling communication between groups that have become mutually isolated and are in conflict with each other. The best negotiations are those in which opportunities are created for both parties to have an informed understanding and appreciation of the reasons for the grievances of the other. In response to "respectful listening" people open themselves up and speak honestly about the issues at stake for them. This setting leads to a genuine sharing of underlying fears, anxieties and reservations. Real issues are brought to the surface and dealt with honestly. True communication takes place in such an environment.

Unfortunately, in much of what is presented as meetings to bring about reconciliation and peace, what we hear are statements made by the parties concerned out of political or diplomatic necessity or, as often admitted, for "public consumption". When real issues are not dealt with and resolved, reconciliation remains too shallow adequately to deal with past misgivings. Such negotiated reconciliation breaks down under the first strain in relationships.

Prejudice – the enemy of communication

Emphasis is placed on mutual trust and on listening and learning because many of the relationships between communities are plagued by prejudices. Prejudice is judgment made without actual knowledge, which one has come to believe to be true. Prejudices are formed in one historical moment and are handed down sometimes through centuries. Prejudices are hard to break and often are denied by those who hold them.

The problem with prejudice, especially in the context of conflict situations, is that specific communities of people are looked at en masse, and as static entities. There is little consideration of developments in the course of history and of how communities might have undergone change as a result. More important, there is very little consideration of the internal diversity that exists within all communities.

Prejudices are also sometimes nurtured and reinforced by careless reporting in the mass media. It is not uncommon, for example, to meet people who regard all Jews as Zionists of a particular variety, or all Palestinians as persons who support violence. In Sri Lanka, some Tamils consider all Sinhalese to be insensitive to the grievances of the Tamils, and some Sinhalese look upon all Tamils as bent on bringing about political change through violent means. An unbelievable level of ignorance and moral blindness besets those who do not recognize and address their own prejudices. Where prejudice is not dealt with, communication hits a stone wall. Even the best-intended actions of a community are treated with doubt and suspicion.

Some believe that prejudices can be removed through education. Although there is truth in this assertion, the best way to deal with prejudice is to enable the communities that are prejudiced against each other to have a new experience of each other. Much emphasis is put in interfaith work on actual meeting between people, on enabling people to speak for themselves, and on empathetic listening to one another, mainly to enable this new experience of the other. Prejudice unfortunately functions like rust, which not only corrupts but also clings to the metal and is not easily removed. Removing prejudice is a challenging process. People whose prejudices have been removed have an experience of re-birth, as it were. The task of communication can ill afford to ignore the role of prejudice in blocking and distorting the channels of communication.

This understanding also shows that communication is what happens between people. Where people in conflict are closed to one another, no amount of communication techniques can help in furthering reconciliation between them.

Communication: a story within a story

Communication strategists sometimes spend enormous time and energy on how to communicate a message, concentrating on the medium used in relation to the people to whom the story is to be told. Here much effort is also invested in creating images, symbols and other forms of communication that would make the story accessible to people in different contexts. This effort is important.

Also important, however, is concentration on the issue of how stories are received by those to whom they are told. All people receive the story that is being told, not in a vacuum, but within their own stories – which take the shape of their cultural and religious life. When communicating in conflict situations, it is therefore perhaps more important to study how the communication would be received by those to whom it is directed, for communication is received, assessed and assimilated within existing stories. Many conflicts arise from the fact that the stories do not connect.

Hindu-Christian relations in India

There is much concern today about the increasing tension, marked also by violence, between the Hindu and Christian communities in India over the issue of conversion. Much of the communication between these communities on the issue does not connect because of the different presuppositions and assumptions that are made. Many Christians have dealt with the issue primarily as an issue of freedom of religion and of respecting the rights of people to remain in, or to convert to, a religion of their choice. They have argued that it is their constitutional right to preach and propagate their faith, and that other citizens have an equally constitutional right to change from one faith to another.

The Hindus do not see this issue as a matter of constitutional rights at all but as an issue of national identity. Hinduism has been a pluralistic religion from the very beginning, with several and sometimes opposing strands of religious traditions within it. It has encompassed many reformation movements within itself. Full-blown religions like Buddhism, Jainism and Sikhism have come out of Hinduism and built up religious communities within the Hindu context, also through a process of convincing others of the truth of their messages. Plurality, witnessing to new spiritual truths, the rising up of new movements and conversions are all part of the Hindu heritage. So why, one would ask, is Hinduism having a difficult time accepting the conversions to Christianity and Islam?

The issue is very complex, especially because it has more recently been mixed up with politics. The use of violence by sections within the Hindu community that are not part of the debate on conversion has also contributed to alienation and polarization, which blurs the discussion.

The classic discussion on conversion within the Hindu context is that Christianity and Islam create communities that are alienated from the culture and religious ethos of India and that these two religions, in the nature of the presentation of their message, challenge the validity of Hinduism and the other religious traditions of India. Hinduism thus experiences Christian and Islamic missions as not playing by the rules of sharing spiritual messages and "converting" from one strand of faith to another as has been practised in India through the ages. This sense of alienation is strengthened by the fact that both Islam and post-colonial Christianity in India arrived with invaders. Hindus are also troubled by the fact that these two communities still have strong financial ties with the corresponding religious groups in lands that conquered India in the past.

Christians and Muslims, for their part, see themselves as true Indians who, despite the differences in religious beliefs, are patriotic to the country. They see no contradiction between their loyalty to the land and their calling it to their way of believing and being. The call by Hindu nationalists to Islam and Christianity to become part of Hinduism is therefore grossly misunderstood by Islam and Christianity as a call to be absorbed into Hinduism. From the Hindu side it is a call to become genuinely Indian in character and ethos and to play the conversion game within the rules of the Indian tradition of mutual respect.

From the Hindu perspective the issue thus has little to do with freedom of religion or the rights of people to have a religion of their choice. Rather, it concerns the assumptions and outcomes in the practice of conversion. If one listened to the protagonists of the two groups, one would become aware of the distinct stories and worldviews within which the messages are received. Misunderstandings grow because of unawareness of the assumptions at work. Where there is no real understanding of the religious and cultural moorings of peoples, communications break down, leading to confusion and conflict.

Returning, then, to the issue of relationship in communication, we should, on the basis of the example above, assert that relationship does not mean maintaining good relations with others but the capacity to see issues as others see them. It has to do with the sensitivity that what we say might be received differently, not because of hostility or ill will, but because it is heard within a different context.

Communication within a cultural and religiously plural world therefore requires the creation of a "culture of dialogue" as the milieu of communication in which the "spirit of dialogue" rules the methods of communication. It is in speaking and listening, giving and receiving, in understanding and being understood that communication takes place across cultural religious traditions. Such communication would create a spirituality of dialogue and cooperation in a world that, despite all the modern tools of communication, is so easily drawn into confrontation and conflict.

Communication, Reconciliation and Religion in America

WILLIAM F. FORE

The definition of reconciliation is to reunite, to restore, to bring people back together. The opposites – separation, estrangement, alienation – are not mere antonyms. They are what bring about the need for reconciliation in the first place. To deal with how communication relates to reconciliation, we must therefore first examine the nature of the alienation. To get at this question, I shall put forward a dozen propositions. Some are fairly commonplace. Others may challenge conventional wisdom and are meant to be somewhat provocative. All will deal with elements in American society that either alienate or restore. Then I shall suggest positive alternatives and strategies.

Proposition 1. Democracy is the social context that best deals with alienation. Alienation occurs between people when there is an intolerable imbalance of power – social, economic or political. Democracy provides the mechanism that involves all participants in deciding who will have what power. Democracy requires that people make their wishes and priorities known, and do so in public forums; it depends on public debate and public scrutiny of the power holders. Democracy thus requires open communication to be available in some degree to every individual. If communication is not freely available, democracy fails. No open communication, no democracy. No open communication, and alienation increases with very little chance for reconciliation.

Proposition 2. Democracy requires confrontation. Confrontation is not necessarily a bad thing. In fact, it is essential to the functioning of the democratic process. As long as confrontation takes place within a context of open and free-flowing communication, it provides the way for people to hear and be heard, to debate and to choose between alternative viewpoints. Confrontation becomes pernicious only when open, two-way communication ceases and violence begins. It becomes dangerous and potentially lethal when the power is held by only one side.

Proposition 3. America is no longer a functioning democracy. As Robert McChesney says in the introduction to his book *Rich Media, Poor Democracy*: "When I invoke the term democracy, then, I mean it in the classical sense, as the rule of the many. A society like the United

States, which has rampant inequality, minimal popular involvement in decision making, and widespread depoliticization can never be regarded as democratic in an honest use of the term."[1] Instead, America today has a kind of pseudo-democracy in which the political system is based on the formal right to vote, but in which the political and economic power is actually closely maintained in the hands of a wealthy few. It is pseudo-democracy in which the political parties serve up Tweedledum-Tweedledee alternatives, with very little to distinguish one position from the other, while candidates engage in TV personality contests and avoid issues as much as possible. The resulting alienation of citizens from the political process has resulted in constantly declining interest in campaigns, issues and voting – all of which plays perfectly into the hands of those who control the levers of power.

Proposition 4. The communication industry plays a major role in creating alienation and defeating the democratic process in America. There are other factors, but the mass media are the most dominant. The US media are an integral part of the capitalist political economy. The hallmarks of this economy are corporate concentration, media conglomeration and hypercommercialism. Here are a few examples of the current media concentration in the United States:

- The five largest music groups account for more than 87 percent of the music market.
- Six firms control more than 80 percent of the cable TV systems.
- Seven firms control 75 percent of the cable programming.
- A few large national chains sell more than 80 percent of all books.[2]

In his book *The Media Monopoly*, Ben Bagdikian wrote in 1983 that some 50 media conglomerates dominated the entire US media scene. By the 1997 edition, however, he wrote that the number had been reduced to about 10, with the prospect of it growing even smaller in the near future.[3]

The alienation caused by the media is best seen in the tremendous barrage of violence on television, cable and film screens. As early as 1985, research conducted by the Annenberg School of Communication for the National Council of Churches revealed conclusively that the viewing of violent TV causes subsequent aggressive behaviour, and that violent sexual material stimulates aggression and sexual violence against women and children.[4] Yet the Center for Communications and Social Policy of the University of California at Santa Barbara reported in 1998 that for the third year in a row violent TV accounted for 60 percent of TV programming.[5]

This alienating process is far more widespread than is generally acknowledged, and far more subtle than mere action violence. Advertising dominates all mass media, and over the past five decades advertising has created a group of world-class shoppers in America who happily accept the dicta that you are what you own, that happiness consists of owning things and that the chief end of human life is the pursuit of this kind of happiness. Of special concern is the success the media have enjoyed in training young people to be consumers, resulting in the rampant commercialization of US childhood. In 1998 revenues from TV advertising specifically aimed at children reached about $1 billion.[6] Each of the four largest US media giants has a full-time children's cable TV channel, with massive advertising aimed at young people 24 hours a day. In addition, commercialism has moved into the public schools. Channel One, an advertising-supported TV programme, provides poor schools with computers, TV sets and access to the Internet. The schools in turn deliver a captive audience of 12 million students – 40 percent of all school children – who every day must watch ten minutes of news programming and two minutes of commercial advertising, on school time.[7]

Commodification of daily life
    This same commercialization has invaded every aspect of daily life. Every organized activity has become commodified. A few examples must suffice. By the 1990s all major sports teams and events had become a part of the commercial media and advertising industries. Today every major media conglomerate owns one or more sports teams. Some 28 sport franchises are controlled by media companies. Top players now regularly expect compensation in the range of millions of dollars per year, plus much more for their endorsements of shoes, automobiles and every other imaginable commercial product. At another level, the whole concept of public parks and spaces is rapidly disappearing from American life as commercialized leisure takes over through the creation of amusement parks. Not only Disney, but also Time Warner and Seagram, three of the largest media conglomerates, now own and operate amusement parks, while public tax spending for public parks has decreased. A more visible presence of the advertising dominance are the hundreds of shopping mall stores now owned by the media giants, which sell dolls, videos and trinkets related to the programmes served up in the guise of entertainment on their television and cable channels.
    Ralph Nader, the Green candidate for president, has remarked that America is now "growing young people up corporate rather than growing them up civic". This observation puts the issue squarely. People who grow up corporate are taught to look inward, to put themselves first, to consume endlessly, to seek out the maximum possible amusement, and to be unconcerned for others, their environment or even the future. Peo-

ple who grow up civic are taught how to relate meaningfully with others, to put the good of the group first, to consume wisely and to use amusement sparingly, and to be concerned for rights of others, for their environment and for the future of humankind. Unfortunately, US media are growing corporate people, with as little civic-mindedness as possible. This trend in turn generates alienation. On the individual level, it creates alienation as people's lives become circumscribed by what they own, which can never be enough, and by entertainment, which can never adequately shield them from life's realities. On the corporate social level it creates intense alienation by abstracting individuals away from others, until they a reach a point where it becomes difficult, if not impossible, for them even to understand the needs and concerns of other people.

Proposition 5. The communication industry suppresses democracy through control of the political process. In its determination to commercialize every aspect of life, the media have turned politics into farce. During the past 30 years, voters have been taught to make judgments about the character and position of candidates without any genuine discussion, on the basis of ten-second sound bites and misleading commercials trivializing their differences and giving limited and prejudicial information. Photo opportunities have replaced points of view, with pictures dominating words because they sell and are cheap to produce. It is now commonplace that the candidate with the most money for media exposure is more than likely to win.

Since the broadcasters are licensed to use scarce channels, however, the public has the right to demand that broadcasters provide programming that meets the public interest, even if it is commercially unattractive. Unfortunately, the media have been remarkably successful in hiding this reality from the public. And since the corporate media control the news and access to the media, they have tremendous power over politicians. For example, Rupert Murdoch was quoted recently as saying he would be willing to keep his Fox News Channel on the air even if it were not profitable, because he wants "the political leverage he can get out of being a major network".[8] Thus the US media system is in the unparalleled position of being able to cover the political debate about its own existence. No other aspect of the capitalist system has quite this degree of clout.

The media have thus become one of the most anti-democratic forces in the nation. Their concentration tends to increase their tendencies towards a profit-driven, advertising-supported media system, which results in hypercommercialism and denigration of journalism and public service. As McChesney says, "It is a poison pill for democracy."[9]

Proposition 6. The media are no longer "American" but have become "global", with America as merely the launching pad. The creation and growth of the multinational corporation is one of the great new factors of our time. While the invention of the corporation at the end of the 19th century gave national entrepreneurs new power without commensurate legal responsibility, the invention of the multinational corporation at the end of the 20th extended both the power and the legal vacuum on their behalf into the whole world. This dominance is nowhere more true than in the expansion and consolidation of the communications media worldwide. Christopher Dixon, director of media research for Paine Webber, a large stockbroker company, said in 1998: "What you are seeing is the creation of a global oligopoly. It happened to the oil and automotive industries earlier this century; now it is happening to the entertainment industry."[10]

Again, here is a thumbnail sketch of the extent of the new global media monopolies:

- The global film industry is the province of seven firms, all of which are parts of larger media conglomerates.
- The global music industry is dominated by five firms, which earn 70 percent of their revenues outside the USA.
- CNN International dominates global TV news, broadcasting in several languages to some 200 nations.
- By 1998 Rupurt Murdoch claimed to have TV networks and systems that reached more than 75 percent of the world's population.
- Three advertising agencies – Omnicom, WPP Group and Interpublic Group – have a combined income greater than the combined income of all other ad organizations worldwide.

This system is characterized by corporations that know no national affiliation or boundaries. Time Warner is earning more than half its income outside the USA, and its shareholders come from all over the world. Bertelsmann, a German multinational, soon expects to have 40 percent of its profits coming from the USA. Four of the eight largest media firms are headquartered outside the United States. However, three of these – News Corp, Sony and Seagram – own three of the major Hollywood film studios. There is no discernible difference in the content of their output, whether they are owned by a majority of shareholders in Japan or Belgium, or have their corporate headquarters in New York or Tokyo. They are not American. They are global.

Proposition 7. The new communication empires are global extensions of the capitalist system, which is inherently anti-democratic and thus deeply alienating. A new kind of quasi-democracy is taking hold that badly distorts the traditional meaning of democracy. It consolidates its power by preaching a mythology that alienates and separates. I have discussed these myths elsewhere.[11] Here I will only list a few. First, the media inculcate certain views about the media themselves:

- The media say they bring us reality, when actually they bring us escape from reality.
- The media say that information overload is inevitable, when it is merely lucrative.
- The media say that the issues of life are simple, yet they are ever more complex.
- The media say that there exists a free flow of information, when there is not.
- In addition, the media tell us things about society in general and "the way things are". This "reality" includes the propositions that efficiency is the highest good, that technology defines society, that the fittest survive, that power rightly belongs with the powerful, that happiness consists of limitless material acquisition, that everything can be purchased, that consumption is an intrinsic good, that wants should be immediately gratified. Finally, the media tell us that the situation is too complex, too ingrained, too powerful to be changed, and that therefore we cannot hope to change it.

This worldview has now become worldwide. It is rapidly taking over local cultures and destroying local values, assumptions and worldviews.

Decline in religious commitment

Proposition 8. America is not a "Christian" nation. This assessment is true at both surface and deeper levels. At the surface level, the old boast about high American church attendance turns out to be untrue. Since the 1960s, some 40 percent of Americans have been telling pollsters that they attended church or synagogue during the last seven days. A recent study, however, based on actual attendance counts in Protestant and Catholic churches, indicates that instead of 40 percent of Protestants attending church on a given Sunday, only about 20 percent do. Instead of 50 percent of Catholics attending church, only 28 percent actually do. In response to criticism from the Gallup Organization, which touted the earlier figures, the authors repeated their research, which reconfirmed their earlier conclusions in both rural and urban settings.[12]

At a deeper level, the picture is more disturbing. The most committed adult Christians in America are found among the cultural Right, those with the least education, the lower half of the income and occupational structure. They tend to be biblical literalists and theological conservatives. They are by far the most addicted to the electronic church, the televangelists who preach all of culture's most pernicious values – mate-

rial success, power, winning, security, wealth. Many of this group have
fallen into the growing alienation and narcissism, the "me-ism" of American individualistic, personalistic, pietistic religion, where sitting in front
of a TV screen becomes an easy alternative to participation in church and
other civic activities.

New Testament scholar John Dominic Crossan has said that whereas
the 20th century saw a fight between religion and science, the 21st century will see a fight between religion and fantasy. By fantasy Crossan
means belief in the magical, the miraculous, involvement in situations
that allow us to avoid facing reality. An obvious illustration of secular
fantasy is Disney World, and all the other "fantasy lands" that are growing rapidly throughout the world. And TV is perhaps the greatest fan-
tasy-supplier of all.

But examples of religious fantasy also abound. The *Christian Century* magazine ran a cartoon showing two people standing in line at a
movie theatre box office. The man says to his companion: "Not me. I go
to see these to get caught up on the issues of our times. For *escape* I go
to church."[13] When Pat Robertson assures a poor woman who is sending
in the money she normally spends for cancer medicine that God will thus
meet all her needs – that is selling fantasy. When Oral Roberts tells his
audience that if they will send in enough money they will get the car, the
house, the success they desire – that is fantasy. When Robert Schuller
interviews the rich and famous at his Crystal Cathedral worship service,
implying that the parishioners may also become rich and famous if they
think positively – that is fantasy too. Meanwhile, the mainline churches
have been haemorrhaging for more than 20 years because middle-class
Americans are finding there less and less relevance to their real lives.

To be sure, there are many thousands of committed, devoted Christians in America. But they are far outnumbered by those who have either
substituted fantasy for authentic religion or who profess no religion at
all. While every person has a religious desire for meaning, this fact does
not necessarily translate into "Christian". It cannot be said today that
America is a Christian nation.

*Proposition 9. America faces a far more serious problem than lack of
church affiliation, namely, radical individualism.* In his book *Habits of
the Heart* (1985), sociologist Robert Bellah wrote about commitment to
community and citizenship in contrast to the growing alienating individualism.[14] More recently, he has characterized the crisis of civic membership as the decline of "social capital", by which he means the networks,
the norms and trust, that hold people together in cooperation to achieve
mutual benefits.[15] His current studies show that the number of people
who say they have recently attended a public meeting for town or school

has fallen by more than one-third since 1973. This growing individualism and alienation is not only social but also individual. The number of people who say that most people can be trusted fell by more than one third between 1960 and 1993. And the "overclass" has also withdrawn from the civic sphere, as indicated by the huge increase in gated, guarded communities for the wealthy.

And what about the youth? Lynn Schofield Clark has explored the role of media in the way teens construct their reality. When teens say they are religious, they may mean that they follow a moral code or that they belong to a church or merely that they have a sentimental feeling of goodness, or else they refer to something that is inexplicable or supernatural in life. They do *not* associate religion as a source of ultimate meaning and purpose for one's life. They pick and choose their religious symbols from TV, from ads – any source. They do *not* relate to formal belief systems or to history, tradition, social justice or community. Their use of religion is "therapeutic and individualistic".[16]

Proposition 10. The people of God, which includes Christians, are facing a radical new world that requires radical new responses. The creation of the global market requires that we think globally. And since the new communication processes play a decisive role in that market, we must deal with it both globally and locally. Although the communication centres of power are no longer merely American, much of their power still operates from America.

At the very least, this capitalist, non-democratic culture must not be allowed to dominate the societies throughout the world. As the large multinational corporations grow in economic and political power, the nation states themselves are inexorably becoming weakened and even dismantled. The alienation that such a culture creates is essentially economic and political in nature and must be dealt with in these terms.

What is the relevance of religion? The insights on economic life that come from the various major religions – Christian, Islamic, Jewish, Confucian and Buddhist – have considerable economic wisdom for the life of people living in community. They can become a rich resource for people to use in organizing their economic life against the global market forces. Yong-Bok Kim, president of Hanil University and Theological Seminary in Korea, has analyzed the biblical vision that bears on this problem. He calls it "the political economy of God", spelled out in the stories of the exodus, the covenant (sabbath), the jubilee, the creation and the new heaven and new earth. For example, Kim refers to the economic manifesto of Jesus in the sixth chapter of Matthew.

Kim calls for the direct intervention and participation of people as citizens in civil society. "A new direct participatory political agency of life and people in local, national and global interconnectedness is being raised and formed everywhere in the world."[17] What is required, says Kim, is for Christians to follow in the tradition of political resistance that has been in place since the beginning of the church.

Proposition 11. At its best, the value of "media diversity" is minimal, and at its worst, it can be diversionary in the attack on media monopoly. Often the idea of media diversity is raised as a major solution to the problem of media monopoly. The use of the Internet, of small local publishing, of audiotapes and street theatre are said to be viable alternatives to the mass media. Yes, they are viable. No, they are not alternatives. They are viable in the sense that the major players of media power ignore and thus tolerate them. They are not alternatives because they are scatter-shot, reaching a tiny minority and then only sporadically. Without systematic and continuous communication, their overall effect is virtually nil.

There are exceptions. When *all* media are completely shut down and tyranny is almost 100 percent, then alternative media can have a significant impact. Witness the value of clandestine presses in South Africa, the use of audiotapes by the followers of Khomeini when he was exiled in Paris, the effect of one FM radio station in Manila during the last days of Marcos. The media monopoly we face today, however, is far more widespread, far more subtle, and therefore far more effective than any blatant dictatorship. It achieves its goals by wooing the crowd, not by intimidating them. George Orwell wrote in his preface to *Animal Farm* that censorship in a "free" society is much more sophisticated and effective than in dictatorships because "unpopular ideas can be silenced, and inconvenient facts kept dark, without any need for an official ban".[18]

Too often, however, media diversity can become a dangerous diversion. We can spend so much time on a hundred small projects that we cannot marshal unified support to attack the underlying systemic causes of alienation. We can busy ourselves trying to reconcile a few, while the need for reconciliation worldwide becomes ever more critical.

Proposition 12. What is needed are strategies that directly challenge the communication monopoly in the global market. The problem I have described is a systemic problem. Getting at systemic problems requires taking action within and against the entire system. Since the problem stems from the social, economic and political system in America, it can be most clearly addressed in America.

Not only do Americans have a unique role to play in dealing with this problem, but so do the American churches. American Christians must deal with the breakdown of democracy and civics *as a religious issue.* For too long Christians have been content to compartmentalize their lives into religious and secular, as though God did not operate equally in both. But the breakdown of democracy is a concrete challenge to God's intention that men and women everywhere should live together in a just and peaceful society. Jesus made this very clear: "Is it not written, 'My house shall be called a house of prayer for all the nations'? But you have made it a den of robbers" (Mark 11:17). As Yong-Bok Kim points out, the Bible is full of stories about the political economy of God, which requires people to live in genuine community, with all that that idea implies. Genuine, open, two-way communication is an essential element in that community, and as long as it is thwarted, God's will for all the people on earth is thwarted. Christians simply cannot turn over the issue of communication policy to "the society". Instead, this issue must become a major element on the agenda of all churches. Having said this, there are several strategies that, while difficult, are practical and effective ones for American Christians to undertake.

Strengthening civil society in the USA

First, American churches should educate their members about their rights as citizens. The broadcast spectrum belongs to the people, and they can determine who uses it, and for what purposes. This fact has been intentionally obscured for so long and so successfully that most citizens now actually believe what the broadcasters tell them: that the stations belong to the broadcasters. Until citizens see this lie for what it is, no meaningful action can be taken.

Second, American churches should insist on immediate campaign-finance reform. In 1998 candidates for political office paid more than $500 million just to buy time on the airwaves. As long as candidates must pay such exorbitant prices even to be heard and seen on radio and TV, the media will continue to exercise its vice-like grip on the political process, and other reforms will be impossible. Commercial broadcasters must be required to provide free airtime for political candidates in exchange for the privilege of holding licenses for which they pay nothing. William Kennard, chairman of the Federal Communication Commission from 1997 to 2001, has made such a proposal, thus far without success. But the public is becoming irate at the soaring costs of political campaigns, and the fact that the FCC itself has raised the question is encouraging. What is not encouraging is that most church groups have remained silent. Instead, they need to exert leadership in building coalitions of community groups to insist that campaign finance reform be enacted.

Once the Gordian knot of campaign costs is cut, the legislators and the administration will be far less beholden to the broadcasting monopolies. At that point, churches can begin to work for additional media reforms such as the following:

1) setting a limit on the number of media outlets a single corporation may control;
2) reducing the amount of commercial time available on radio and TV;
3) requiring a fixed amount of TV and radio time for children's programming, with no commercials;
4) restricting the time of day when programmes with heavy violence and sexual violence can be shown;
5) regulating the rates of cable systems, which use the public streets, and satellite systems, which use the public spectrum;
6) creating adequate funding for public broadcasting, through such mechanisms as a dedicated tax (not subject to annual congressional approval) on TV sets or on the profits of commercial broadcasters;
7) restricting the amount of American-based programming available for export each year.

These strategies seem visionary at present, and they may not be enacted for many years to come. But the alternative is unacceptable: a world dominated by less than half-a-dozen huge conglomerates, which become the only sources for news and entertainment for the entire global population. That virtual monopoly would create the kind of future envisioned by Aldous Huxley in *Brave New World*, in which the seemingly benign technologies of radio, TV and film provide everyone everywhere with the politics of image, news as entertainment, and important social and economic issues carefully obscured by trivia, so that everyone is grown up corporate, no one is grown up civic, and civil society simply ceases to exist. In that situation, reconciliation becomes impossible.

These are profoundly religious matters, and American Christians have a unique responsibility towards them – first, because the problems are rooted in America, and second, because God needs their response as never before.

NOTES

[1] Robert W. McChesney, *Rich Media, Poor Democracy*, Urbana, Univ. of Illinois Press, 1999, p.5.
[2] *Ibid.*, pp.17-18.
[3] Ben Bagdikian, *The Media Monopoly*, 5th ed., Boston, Beacon Press, 1997.
[4] "Violence and Sexual Violence in Film, Television, Cable and Home Video", report of a study committee of the Communication Commission, National Council of Churches of Christ in the USA, 1985, p.5.
[5] Christopher Stern, "Researchers Shocked to Find – TV Violence", *Variety*, 20-26 April 1998, p.24.
[6] Jim McConville, "Higher Stakes in Kids Cable Battle", *Electronic Media*, 17 Nov. 1997, pp.3,63.
[7] Channel One Network advertisement, *Electronic Media*, 8 February 1999, p.36.

[8] Chuck Ross, "From the Top of TCI", *Electronic Media*, 29 Sept. 1997, p.50.

[9] McChesney, *Rich Media*, p.2.

[10] Emma Duncan, "Wheel of Fortune", *Economist*, 21 Nov. 1998, "Technology and Entertainment Survey", *ibid.*, p.4.

[11] William F. Fore, *The Mythmakers: Gospel, Culture and Media*, New York, Friendship Press, 1990, pp.52-56.

[12] C. Kirk Hadaway and P.L. Marler, "Did You Really Go To Church This Week? Behind the Poll Data", *Christian Century*, 6 May 1998, pp.472-75.

[13] *Christian Century*, 1 March 1989, p.225.

[14] Robert Bellah, et al, *Habits of the Heart*, Berkeley, Univ. of California Press, 1985.

[15] Robert Bellah et al., "Individualism and the Crisis of Civic Membership", *Christian Century*, 20-27 March 1996, p.260.

[16] Lynn Schofield Clark, "Exploring the Role of Media in Religious Identity-construction among Teens", Religion Online website, May 1998.

[17] Yong-Bok Kim, "Civil Society: Unity and Oikos – the House of God", Religion Online website.

[18] Quoted in John Pilger, *Hidden Agenda*, London, Vintage, 1998, p.468.

Communication and Reconciliation with Truth

DAFNE SABANES PLOU

They think you've died because they've killed you.
They think they can cut down the woods with one blow of an axe.
They might even think that we are here to lament your death.
Because what they don't know, really, is that you have multiplied.
That you are looking through all our eyes, speaking through our mouths,
Hugging with our arms,
Walking in all our footsteps.

Mothers of the Plaza de Mayo, Founding Charter

If anything characterized the military dictatorship that governed Argentina between 1976 and 1983 it was silence, governed by terror. Fear of speaking; fear of seeing; fear of having information; fear of writing; fear of denouncing the outrages; fear of reading; fear of possessing books, publications and notes, which led hundreds of people to burn their libraries and archives; fear of demonstrating commitment to the defence of human rights that were systematically violated from the first day of the coup. Fear imposed silence, but silence was initially imposed through persecution, forced disappearances, concentration camps, torture, murder and exile for political opponents, all carried out with impunity by the oppressors.

For silence about what was going on to be complete, however, it was necessary for the dictatorship "to disappear" 84 journalists, whose fate still remains unknown, and to kill, persecute and provoke the exile of many more. Prior censorship got the better of all the media, and even those in private hands scarcely mentioned the disappearance and murder of thousands of citizens. Self-censorship reigned in editors' offices, and freedom of the press was violated thousands of times, as were the human rights of a people who, in many cases, preferred to ignore the horror of what was happening on a daily basis.

The mass media run by the dictatorship fostered lying and concealment. While the authorities distributed self-adhesive stamps with the words "We Argentines are upright and human" in order to counter, so people said, the anti-Argentine defamation campaign that political opponents were promoting outside the country, the mass media increased people's suspicion and rejection of the victims of state terrorism. They spread the idea that "there must have been some reason" for their disappearance, for them to have died in a hail of bullets, for their bodies to have been blown up with dynamite, for the security forces to have torn down and ransacked the homes and belongings of the detained and disappeared. The victims were tried and found guilty by meticulous, convincing and aggressive opinion makers. A new generation of journalists devoted its time to justifying the dictatorship, while radio and television studios were filled with favourable coverage of those responsible. The dictatorship sent out messages that made fathers suspect their own children and instructed people how to keep an eye on the way young people behaved, because in each one there could be hidden an "enemy of the mother country". In this way they ensured that the veil of silence surrounding violations of human rights thickened and became almost impenetrable.

Meanwhile the relatives of the disappeared went from public office to public office seeking information about the whereabouts of their loved ones. They also went to the police stations, to the armed forces' units and to the bishops and priests who held posts in the military sphere and even to the apostolic nuncio. There was no response to their cries. Nobody seemed to know or to be concerned about what was really going on. One day at Government House, at the very heart of power, while they were waiting to be seen by the authorities, a group of women decided to go public with their situation. They thought that it no longer made sense to go on privately knocking on office doors but that their pleas would surely gain strength from being made publicly known. They were courageous. As their meeting place they chose the Plaza de Mayo (May Square), in front of Government House, a locale that throughout Argentine history was the scene of great social and political demonstrations, some of which caused substantial changes in the country's direction.

The mothers kept each other informed by telephone and thus set up the beginnings of a chain of communication. Those that came to the square that first day were little more than a dozen. It was 30 April 1977. The dictatorship was more than one year old, and oppression against opponents was severe. Azucena Villaflor, one of the many mothers who was desperately seeking her disappeared children, led the meeting. It was an informal chat during which the mothers compared notes on their situation, stated their problems and concerns, and decided to continue meeting each week to strengthen their public appeal. In the name of thousands of missing persons, they established a presence before dictators, who tried to drown oppression in oblivion and to impose "unmemory" by means of paralysing fear.

At first the group passed unnoticed. But as the number of mothers and other relations grew at the weekly rendezvous, the authorities began to take measures to prevent them from meeting. The dictatorship prohibited citizens from gathering in groups in public places, so the mothers began walking through the square in threes and fours. Thus began their famous rounds, which concentrated on the May Pyramid, symbol of freedom and independence. Gradually they took the name "Mothers of the Plaza de Mayo". On the one hand, respect and admiration grew for the silent struggle of this group of women who every Thursday were brave enough to point out human rights violations in the face of power. On the other hand, a campaign of suspicion was organized against these "mothers of subversives", these "mad women from the square", who "must have done something" to find themselves in such a situation.

The Mothers of the Plaza de Mayo, and then the Grandmothers of the Plaza de Mayo (an association created a few months later to search for the hundreds of children kidnapped with their parents or born in captivity), consolidated their position by publicizing their complaints in the most public and symbolic of places. Perhaps it would not have concerned the dictatorship greatly that a group of middle- and lower-class housewives met every week to cry about their misfortunes. But the Mothers and Grandmothers worked for human rights not with the tearful demeanour of victims but with the strength of calling into question and denouncing the outrages of a power that seemed implacable. The Mothers and Grandmothers arose as credible, trustworthy and solid subjects of communication. They wore white scarves on their heads during their weekly rounds, on which they had sewn names of children and family members who had been detained or disappeared. These headscarves became symbols of a denunciation that penetrated looks and minds. The message of the Mothers and Grandmothers was stronger and more persuasive than all the propaganda broadcast by radio and television, the brightly lit advertising posters, the military marches and speeches calling for patriotism, the authoritarianism and terror of the dictatorship.

The work of other human rights organizations set up during this period confirmed reports of the serious violations of human rights and the terrible oppression that the Argentine people suffered. Nothing was easy for these groups, which were also persecuted. Azucena Villaflor herself, along with a group of mothers and other persons who supported her demands, disappeared at the end of 1977. It was a harsh blow for the human rights movement, but the force of their demands did not diminish but continued growing even during the hardest times of oppression. The cover-up had begun to be exposed, and through this small beginning many people, inside and outside the country, began to realize the true situation of oppression, disappearances and cruel subjection that already involved thousands of people from all sectors of society – children, young people, men and women of all ages, including the disabled, and infants born in captivity.

Gestating communication for truth

Lacking access to the mass media, the human rights organizations established in Argentina in the 1970s created their own networks of alternative communication to reach the people with real information about what was going on in the country. Besides denunciations in international forums and appeals to public opinion abroad, it was also necessary to do the important work of conscientization among Argentines themselves, to banish the suspicions raised by the dictatorship about everyone who took part in the struggle and to allay the fears that prevented getting nearer to the truth.

The division created by the dictatorship in the nation was such that when Adolfo Pérez Esquivel received the Nobel Peace Prize in 1980 many felt insulted and rejected the notion that an architect unknown to the majority could receive such an important award, having committed himself to a cause whose existence was being questioned by public opinion. Who were these defenders of human rights? What did they want? To ruin the country with their criticisms? Many hesitated to denounce the military for their enormous crimes, not wanting to attack those who for decades had presented themselves as "saviours of the nation", taking government in successive coups d'état in order to correct "mistakes" made by civilians. It was difficult to think about the existence of another Argentina when the mass media only reinforced the military power with its messages.

The opportunity finally arose in 1982 after the defeat of the military in the Malvinas/Falklands War. Together the human rights organizations decided to organize a huge march through the streets of Buenos Aires to appeal on behalf of the disappeared, who at that time were estimated to number 30,000 people. A mass, public act was needed that would once again occupy a symbolic space, such as May Avenue, which linked Government House at one end with the National Congress at the other. The message had to be clear: the reality of the disappeared and the human rights violations had to be fearlessly proclaimed in the very nerve centre of Argentina, in the avenue that linked executive power, at that time usurped, with legislative power, at that time prescribed, in a powerful call to unmask those responsible and at the same time demand truth and justice.

It was expected that the procession would leave from one of the busiest corners of the city and reach the Plaza de Mayo to demonstrate there. At the appointed time many uniformed police were in evidence at the agreed place, and others were certainly present in civilian clothing, but there were only a few demonstrators spread about, alone or in small groups, as if passing the time. But when the head of the procession appeared, with members of religious orders, political personalities and leaders of human rights movements in front, then thousands of people seemed to come out of nowhere, joining the march in close order, adding a strength of voices, chants and a firm step, giving it impulse and a power of denunciation that was difficult to avoid. The police tried to block their advance but had to give way before a force of such size. Even though they diverted the procession through adjacent streets to prevent the demonstrators from reaching the Plaza de Mayo, the police did not act repressively. The demonstration was totally non-violent. What was interesting about it was that as it advanced, it was supported by people who came to windows and onto balconies and pavements to accompany the marchers with their silent, somehow respectful, presence, adding a clamour that echoed off the walls of the tall buildings – "Tell us where the disappeared are: with life you took them, with life we want them."

The march generated the hoped for communication. The following day the media could not deny its existence. According to the official account, of doubtful objectivity, some 10,000 people took part in an act that marked the end of a long and enforced public silence. They did not reach the square because the police stopped them, and the leaders at the head of the procession chose to ask the demonstrators to disperse peacefully, though they first staged a memorable sit-down just a few metres from Government House. It was the first mass call to the consciences of many and a signal to the dictatorship and people that no further concealment was possible and that the moment of truth, sooner or later, would arrive.

The striking thing about this process of communication for truth that began in Argentina with the rounds of the Mothers and Grandmothers of the Plaza de Mayo, silent but loaded with symbolism and denunciation, was that it came from below, from newly founded social movements and networks that lifted up the very bonds of solidarity, mutual trust and hope that the dictatorship tried to bury. The churches and the ecumenical movement played their part in this movement. Just as human rights groups began with involvement by political and social leaders, so did various Protestant and Evangelical churches, a handful of brave Catholic dioceses and leaders of these churches and of the Jewish community take part in two organizations: the Permanent Assembly for Human Rights, and the Ecumenical Movement for Human Rights. The world ecumenical movement, through the Office of Human Rights for Latin America of the World Council of Churches, gave strong support to human rights work in Argentina both at the technical and the reporting levels in international forums and in the financing of work carried out by these organizations. Ecumenical funds especially supported the task of finding children born in captivity, carried out by the Grandmothers of the Plaza de Mayo.

The presence of people of religion from different churches and beliefs who had worked together during the worst years of oppression, heading the march organized by all the organizations in 1982, gave moral and ethical support to the call for truth and justice. Their participation also gave rise to deep theological reflection from a Latin American perspective on the struggle to defend human rights and the commitment that comes from the gospel. Interwoven with liberation theology, such reflection pervaded the work of numerous priests, pastors, members of religious orders and believers who committed themselves ecumenically to this work. Some of them appear on the lists of those who disappeared or were victims of the oppression in Argentina, and many others had to go into voluntary exile.

This phenomenon was repeated in many Latin American countries that faced similar situations of oppression, state terrorism and human rights violations. In a thousand and one ways social bonds were forged in support of a cause that affected everyone and united them in the search for a greater good. In the case of the Mothers and Grandmothers, meetings with mothers from other countries who had also experienced the forced disappearance of their children and loved ones led to the emergence of similar groups in various Latin American and Asian countries and similar support in solidarity from other organizations of civil society.

With the arrival of democracy, communication channels opened to the search for truth in Argentina. The new government, headed by Raúl Alfonsín, gave impulse to the chief initiative: the creation of the National Commission on the Disappearance of Persons (CONADEP) to investigate human rights violations during the dictatorship. Two years later, this investigation became the basis of legal charges brought against members of the military juntas that had exercised power for seven years. The trial ended with the indefinite imprisonment of several of the worst members of the dictatorship, who were found guilty of murder, torture and the forced disappearance of individuals. It is noteworthy that among the ten members of CONADEP were three religious figures: two bishops, Carlos Gattinoni (Methodist) and Jaime de Nevares (Catholic), and a rabbi, Marshall Meyer, all of them militant supporters of human rights and very active in their commitment during the dictatorship

An interesting communication process began at this stage, which now involved various media, both public and private. It broadened to include eyewitness testimony given before the members of CONADEP by victims of oppression, exiles, family members and close friends of those disappeared and murdered by the dictatorship, as well as by former oppressors who had now repented; public visits to the secret detention centres and concentration camps where thousands of political prisoners had suffered every kind of torture and death; the drawing up of *Nunca más* (Never again), the official report of CONADEP; and the filming and later broadcasting of the trial of the military juntas. The media responded in full to the need to inform people of what had really happened and to the deep desire to find the truth, those responsible for violations, and to do justice.

It was not by chance that *Nunca más* became a huge best-seller. The *Trial Daily*, published during the trial of the military juntas, with transcriptions of the testimonies given by victims of the oppression, sold out every day. Nor was it by chance that the film *The Official Story* (winner of an Oscar for Best Foreign Film), portraying the illegal appropriation of children by the oppressors, brought tens of thousands of people into the cinemas. Debates on the subject took place on radio and television, and the public became more and more aware of the need to recover memory and to remain firm in denouncing what had happened so that it would not recur and future generations would be free of persecution, imprisonment and oppression for political reasons.

With the re-establishment of democracy, the mass media, above all the newspapers and magazines, took the subject of human rights as one of their main topics of information and investigative journalism. New publications and periodicals were created. The journalists who came back from exile, as well as many others who had had no editorial role during the dictatorship, contributed with their reflections and analysis to ending the silence and bringing information to light that had remained hidden for many years and was at risk of being destroyed or lost for ever. The democratic press played an important role in the consolidation of a new culture of human rights that, although initially limited to violations carried out by the dictatorship, was later broadened to include issues related to greater social, economic, political and civil participation.

But the springtime of democracy in Argentina could not last long. Checked by the military, who saw its chiefs of staff imprisoned and whose new leaders ran the risk of experiencing the same fate, by the structural adjustment programmes of the International Monetary Fund and by economic and financial crises, the government weakened and gave way to various pressures that impeded the judging of intermediate-level military and police personnel who had acted wrongfully during the oppression but who were denying their responsibility by saying that they were simply carrying out the orders of their superiors. Faced with an attempted military coup in Holy Week 1987 that put the incipient democracy in danger, the people showed how far the message had sunk in of *Nunca más* and the advocacy of the Mothers and Grandmothers during their weekly rounds, with the dozens of other organizations, political parties, personalities, representatives of churches and social movements.

The oppressors managed to pass a law of "Due Obedience", which exempted them from being tried. The majority of civilians, however, were convinced of the military's responsibility for the human rights violations and understood that it must always be kept away from political power. People poured into the streets, accompanied by their children, surrounded the barracks, and fearlessly berated the military chiefs face to face, in the deep conviction that they did not want to lose their hard-won democracy. Truth had won its place in their minds. Although the offenders were not judged completely, the military had lost the trust and prestige with which it had cloaked itself in other times. Its leaders came to see the rejection and condemnation they had provoked in ordinary citizens.

What reconciliation are we talking about?

In December 1990 the government presided over by Carlos Menem decided to pardon the chiefs of the military dictatorship, alleging the need to "reconcile" the country. Those pardoned were widely rejected by society, public opinion, the human rights movements both in Argentina and abroad, and many politicians. Refusing to go back on its decision, the government tried to establish a sort of national reconciliation. It existed only in official pronouncements, however, and was otherwise ephemeral. People widely felt there was no good reason for this presidential decision, other than carrying out some secret pact with the military to end the imprisonment of these high-ranking officers. The discourse of reconciliation, which was even endorsed by some members of the Catholic Church hierarchy, gained no ground among the people, who, supported by the human rights organizations, responded with a mass march against those pardoned.

The wounds made by the oppression were still open, and it became impossible to talk about reconciliation when military pronouncements continued justifying the "war against subversion". Despite the atrocities committed, those in political power refused to ensure that justice would be meted out to all those responsible for the oppression.

The members of the military juntas regained their freedom, but not their acceptance by society. On more than one occasion they were booed in the street, the same as other notorious oppressors might be, with the people demonstrating the vividness of their memories and their fearless dignity. With the coming of other problems, however, such as the acute economic crisis, unemployment and political corruption, people gradually lost interest in questions of human rights linked to violations committed during the military dictatorship.

What was needed was active advocacy, especially by the Mothers and Grandmothers of the Plaza de Mayo, to keep the memory of these events alive and to continue seeking the truth about the disappearance of individuals – in particular, the whereabouts of the almost 500 children who disappeared with their parents or were born in captivity. Many of these babies were given to families of the oppressors through illegal adoption. This crime was proved by the Grandmothers of the Plaza de Mayo, who, using such new technologies of communication as the Internet and e-mail, found and recovered about 65 children, some of whom were officially registered as children of military or police officers.

Reconciliation with the truth

Were the people aware of what was really going on during the years of the dictatorship? Or were the majority perhaps not bothered that human rights were being systematically violated in the country, or that a plan existed for the annihilation of political opposition, even including newborn babies? A large part of the population likely did not know the reality of the oppression, and another part likely bought the official line, believing the censored information broadcast by the dictatorship-dominated mass media. Some justified the "struggle against subversion", although they never had clear insight into the horrors that existed in the concentration camps and secret prisons. Others preserved an image of the military as untainted by corruption, thinking they could be oppressors without being crooks, and years later found it hard to accept the revelation that some of them had large accounts in Swiss banks.

Committed and courageous work by hundreds of men and women with deep respect for human rights succeeded in preventing the dictatorship from drowning out memory, distorting the meaning of justice and burying truth with deception. Throughout the dictatorship years, the human rights organizations set themselves up as ethical bastions that knew how to keep in their hearts the ideals they thought had been lost. After seven years of dictatorship, the Argentine people had to reconcile themselves to the truth. They had to face the long lists of those murdered and disappeared, of political prisoners and exiles, and also to acknowledge the existence of concentration camps, clandestine prisons, secret graves, hidden births, and concealed torture cells.

This uncovering of the truth, achieved through marches, denunciations, symbolic acts, non-violent resistance and an all-out militancy in support of justice, established a consensus in society that allowed many people to recover the trust and solidarity that the dictatorship sought to destroy. It also enabled them to testify about clues, signs, suspicions about situations related to the forced disappearance of people or children. This consensus, which was also created abroad, led to steps being taken in various countries to try Argentine oppressors for their role in the disappearance of nationals who had been living in Argentina. Moreover, this persistent work succeeded by the end of the 1990s in ensuring that various members of the military juntas and other oppressors were detained once again for the robbery and change of legal identity of minors, a crime not covered by the law of "Due Obedience".

On 24 March 1996, fully 20 years after the military coup, a huge march took place through the central streets of Buenos Aires to the Plaza de Mayo to commemorate the victims of the dictatorship and to condemn those who were responsible for it. On that day a new human rights group made its first public appearance: HIJOS, made up of hundreds of young people, the children of political prisoners, disappeared persons, exiles and themselves also victims of the dictatorship. The birth of this organization was a sign of hope, for now memory would not be lost but would continue alive. Alongside these young people, who in many ways had suffered the oppression themselves, thousands more filled the square because they had full knowledge of what had happened in their country. They said "never again", convinced that it would be necessary to carry on fighting for greater justice and that living with the truth makes people and nations honourable and free.

Communication Ethics
with a Pluralist Worldview

TISSA BALASURIYA O.M.I.

Ethics deals with the principles and norms of conduct, the right and wrong or morality of human action. The principles of ethics can be determined by the nature, purpose and consequences of a human act or they may be garnered from the teaching of a philosophy or religion such as Christianity. Ethical principles depend on the understanding of the goal of human life, first, as known by natural reason, and second, as held by a philosophy or religion.

We can distinguish the content of ethical positions and the motivation for accepting them. The same content can be accepted for different motives, or one motive can give different ethical contents according to the contexts and understanding of issues. The motive may determine the content, as when one chooses an action out of love of neighbour. One's worldview may give the motivation for one's action.

Christian morality is linked to the view of God as creator of the whole human race and thus the idea that the resources of the earth are meant for the fulfilment of all humans. This position is supported by the clear teaching of Jesus Christ that God is love and that we must love one another as he has loved us. The love of God is realized and expressed through the love of the neighbour, especially anyone in need.

Morality in this perspective is the law of God, though it would be understood differently in different contexts. The life, teaching and example of Jesus and the belief that the Spirit of God inspires all towards the good – love, truth, justice and peace – is a powerful motivation for such other-centred moral behaviour and links religion to morality. Recent renewal of Christian moral theology has insisted on the primacy of the call of Christ to loving service of all, over and above some conclusions from philosophy or natural law, and more than the rigid demands of canon law.

Communication ethics

Since communications are very important for the formation of worldviews, the ethics guiding communications has a very important significance for the relationships among groups. People's actions depend on their perceptions and values, which are based on the information communicated to them. This information in turn can lead to changes in relationships and structures of society. Social revolutions such as those in France in 1789 and in Russia in 1917 have been triggered by views communicated to peoples.

The world reality has always been pluralist, divided principally according to gender, race and ethnicity, language and culture, religion, nationality, class and life-style. We can distinguish between plural worldviews (made up of several particularist worldviews) and a pluralist worldview, which considers humankind as one family and inhabiting one world, though made up of several differing groups. A pluralist worldview would not consider one people or their own values as necessarily more important than those of others. Historically, most humans have not had a pluralist worldview in that they have not recognized or respected many other aspects of this diversity, as they lived within their own narrow confines and knew or thought little of others. They often considered their own community as the main reality on earth. Others were less important or were considered alien or even subordinate to them.

Formerly prevalent worldviews were generally particularist, partial and exclusivist. These were sometimes supported by metaphysical or theological presuppositions concerning the importance of one's own community. Thus Catholic Christians, for example, considered themselves as more loved or provided for by God for eternal salvation. (This view was recently expressed again, in September 2000, in the declaration *Dominus Jesus* of the Vatican Congregation for the Doctrine of the Faith.)

Though in earlier times the peoples had different worldviews, their exclusivity and intolerance did not impinge much on each other, as communications were limited. Exceptions, however, were the worldwide exploitation of women, the enslaving of peoples, caste and racial discrimination, colonial conquests and religious crusades.

A communications ethic with a pluralist worldview

Content. Ethical norms with reference to message or the content of communication depend on the nature and function of communications. Communications are meant to give information, to educate and entertain persons and groups and build understanding in human community. The content communicated should be truthful and not false, or destructive of desirable human values. Communication should help develop more informed, truthful, just, peaceful and cultured persons and communities. For this effect to happen, misunderstandings and prejudices should be removed, and right relationships fostered.

In a pluralist worldview opportunities must be provided for differing perspectives to be expressed, especially for the poor and oppressed to articulate their point of view. Otherwise truth and fair play may not be served, and conflicts may be increased. This provision is particularly required in situations of confrontation, as the opposing side may be demonized, as happened to the Jews under Hitler and to the Vietnamese and Iraqis in the US wars against them. The information communicated must advance genuine freedom, justice and the equitable sharing of the resources of the earth among all peoples and foster a healthy development of economy and society.

These ethical norms should be guidelines for media personnel such as journalists, media producers, owners of news agencies, including media conglomerates, as well as for nation-states and the world community. The readership and audiences can help realize the norms by their judicious patronage and the creation of public opinion.

Motivation. Communications should be motivated towards reaching these goals of the human common good. The primacy of a motivation such as profit maximization for the owners, producers of communication or the artists and journalists would not be a good ethical norm. Communication may be used to increase profit of businesses as by advertisements. The quest of profits, however, should not be at the expense of the truth, the common good or the moral values of society.

Lamentably, many of the modern communications media seek profit by presenting sex, violence and sensationalism and by arousing popular passions, as in ethnic conflicts. The media are often used to build suspicion, jealousy, hatred and enmity among peoples and sometimes even to encourage wars. The media often aggravate conflicts, thus benefiting arms producers and sellers, and prevent their peaceful resolution by appealing to national pride, historical antagonisms, religious rivalries and cultural hostilities. Furthermore, with the possibility of military commands from afar, communications are now a primary weapon in warfare.

Ownership of the media of communications. For better or for worse, communications now depend very much on modern technology such as computers, TV, satellites and related equipment. Consequently, the production of programmes requires much finance and expensive research and development. Large-scale networks are required for making them efficient and viable. The world market for telecommunications and broadcasting satellites is dominated by the developed countries. Their giant multinational corporations, controlling much of world trade, influence the content of the media through advertisements.

Since the ownership of the means of communication is concentrated in the hands of a few persons, companies or countries (e.g. Rupert Murdoch, Ted Turner), it is their point of view that is presented by the media of communications. The communications business itself is helping to create a few such multibillionaires as Bill Gates of Microsoft.

The oligopolistic worldwide news agencies can influence information and human consciousness extremely swiftly and globally. They have benefited from the dominant capitalistic socio-economic system and in turn support its worldview that the so-called free market brings about the best ordering of world society. Their primary motivation is profits for themselves rather than truth, justice and right relationships among peoples. For the sake of profits they pander to the market of people's passions and popular prejudices.

Media workers such as journalists, scriptwriters and artists have to accept the priorities of the advertisers and owners of the media. They must submit their talents, and sometimes even their conscience, to such priorities.

Forms of censorship are another means by which the media services are made subject to the powers that be. Censorship may be necessary in certain circumstances, such as to protect due privacy, and also to prevent the escalation of conflicts. But censorship is generally used by dictatorial authorities to prevent criticism of their abuses of power.

Positive impact. Modern means of communication and interaction have positively contributed to the making of a pluralist worldview that recognizes the existence and rights of many groups, nations, cultures and religions. They have helped develop considerably the consciousness of the dignity of others, not limited to the values or presuppositions of one's own group only. Technological advances like the Internet provide for the communication of news and views without easy control by public authorities. This freedom can help in the organization of peoples' struggles for justice.

Modern communications permit a greater worldwide freedom of expression. Dictatorships find it more difficult to suppress human rights and control the media of communication. The claims of having a monopoly on the truth or the good, as by a religion like Christianity, a philosophy such as Marxism or an ideology like free-enterprise capitalism, are more easily contested and countered. The harm caused to health, economy or ecology by agencies such as transnational corporations (TNCs) can be exposed and campaigned against globally.

Negative impact. The control over wealth brings about a quasi monopoly of information, research and communications. The powerful rich who control the means of communication decide what to present to the whole world as information and what to gloss over or obliterate from people's awareness or memory. They can condition people's thinking by filtering information to suit their interests. Attractive media are used to distract the attention of people almost everywhere from much-needed radical social changes. The goals of communication media are thus warped to support the dominant system.

The mass of information available can make for a superficiality and a diversion from the deeper realities instead of their critical evaluation. Citizens are conditioned to be passive, to work, trade, consume and be distracted from those deeper realities and to consider the possession of material goods as the goal of human life. This conditioning leads to a culture of selfishness and self-gratification, at the cost of others, nature and the future. There is a commercialization of art, music, entertainment, leisure, sports, scientific research and even religion, a sort of prostitution of the intellect and spirit.

With globalization a worldwide monoculture tends to impose itself on all peoples, proposing one set of values to all peoples. This single culture is symbolized by McDonald's, Coca-Cola and pop music. The theory of the benefits of the "free market" provides the ideological justification for this global trend. There is certainly much resistance to this uniformity by people's movements throughout the world.

While the majority of the world's people are immensely exploited by the rich classes, powerful groups and countries, there is a conscious or unconscious cover-up of this situation. The interests of the rich determine the content of communication. The interests of the poor, the weak and the oppressed are neglected. The media can conveniently ignore issues that the powerful do not want to consider, such as the distribution of land and population, and the debt owed by the former colonizers to the colonized.

Globalization tends towards a homogenization of thinking, even among many academics and policy advisers. Many of these people surmise that there is no alternative to this globalization, or no alternative market for their talents in the global market. The UN system and its powerful International Monetary Fund (IMF) and World Bank are also very much under the domination of the rich of the world. The research and development universities are also rather dependent on big finance and now increasingly under the influence of the very rich companies located mainly in the rich countries.

The provisions of the World Trade Organization for the preservation of intellectual property rights, as through patents, under the auspices of the UN agencies, are said to be meant to encourage creativity of inventors, but they often disadvantage the poor. Their rich treasure of traditional knowledge such as of indigenous medicine and traditional seeds are patented with minor changes by big TNCs. Patents are a means through which there is a considerable transfer of funds from the poor to the rich. The sharing in scientific advancement and its benefits is dependent very much on the economic standing of the different countries and the people. The transfer of technology does not take place except at a price. The poor bear much of the unfavourable effects of technological development such as environmental pollution.

Freedom of communication. The UN Declaration of Human Rights fosters the democratic rights of freedom of opinion, association and of religion. "Everyone has the right to freedom of thought, conscience and religion... of opinion and expression... of peaceful assembly and association" (arts 18-20).

These rights are most valuable for the formation of public opinion. Merely affirming the rights, however, cannot lead to changes in mentalities, relationships and global structures for justice. Just as the "free market" does not lead to economic justice against the background of grave inequalities, so freedom of communication does not lead to the needed communication of information and changes in values because of imbalances in ownership of the means of communication. Furthermore, national security states often control people's freedom of expression so severely that there is little or no possibility of speaking out against the injustices of the prevailing social order.

While the right is expressed to "freely participate in the cultural life of the community", there is no indication as to what this cultural life is to be, due probably to the multicultural nature of the world and of states. It does not necessarily mean that the quality of life of the persons or the community is thereby improved. Much depends on the content of a culture, especially the values it embodies and communicates to successive generations. Capitalistic globalization knows how to operate successfully, supporting the freedom of individuals and associations but preserving the values of capitalistic globalization, which foster the accumulation of wealth, even while the poverty of others increases.

Alongside the explosion of information due to the media, there is a colossal ignorance among those most open to the media because of the impact of prejudice, or preconceptions, and control of information and of educational systems. Thus peoples in the West, including the USA, are rather ignorant about their role in setting up and benefiting from the prevalent cruel world system that we have called global apartheid. The very surfeit of news hides the deeper issues and even foils any efforts at changing the world order for a better distribution of resources among peoples.

The world reality

Beyond the talk of world development, what exists today is a white, racist world order of nation-states built up during the past five centuries by the West, mainly by force. It is guaranteed by the military power of the USA and western Europe and their domination of the UN Security Council. The global economic system is dominated by capitalist values and the TNCs. The media are controlled by a few capitalist megacorporations, which in turn inspire a monoculture dominated by the West. Males dominate in almost all cultures and countries. The environment is being threatened by a wasteful life-style.

These issues need reconciliation among the peoples of the world and within communities. In somewhat earlier times there were norms that public authorities and social pressure tried to enforce on the media for the common good of society and to avoid scandal for children. Now with the prevalence of the ideology of the "free market", it is often argued that market demand and supply would regulate the media. This regulation does not include moral norms that are made binding by a local or global public authority. The technological nature of the means of communication such as the Internet may make such control ineffective or less effective.

Over a few decades communications may bring changes in values and mind-sets of people at a local and even a national level on issues such as caste, class and ethnic relations, especially where the political groups in power favour such an evolution. The public authorities and civil society agencies can be more effective on issues such as environment that affect both the rich and the poor. But they are less effective on issues such as poverty eradication, avoiding of violence and pornography for profit. There is no serious interest regarding global economic justice or white racism, for the status quo benefits the dominant. Internationally, how can the large new global agencies be made accountable for their use of the media of communications? Their worldviews are not necessarily pluralist, though they may operate in many environments and cultures, and almost universally and 24 hours a day, as CNN endeavours to do.

No authorities can impose moral norms on these agencies. Nation-states cannot control these giant media empires through legislative, executive or judicial authority. Nor is there an effective international body for this purpose. The UN as it is presently conceived and structured is not capable of finding meaningful solutions for this evil.

World apartheid and reconciliation facing the 21st century

To understand the difficulties involved, we can take one issue: the just distribution of population in the world's land spaces. The present land possessions of nation-states are regarded as a legitimate right of dominant peoples and are backed by the UN system and the armed force of the superpowers.

A basic factor surrounding the entire issue of communications is the prevailing world apartheid. Apartheid is a system or social order in which there is an imposition of superiority of one group over others, as was in South Africa. During these centuries enormous resources, including gold and silver, were transported from the colonies to the colonizing nations. This movement helped in the development of Western capitalism and in building its economic power base.

This global apartheid is one of our biggest structural evils. It is the result of Western colonial invasions and genocide, carried on by force from generation to generation since 1492 and consolidated by the victors in terms of territorial frontiers. It is racist to an extreme degree, leading to Western fear of the disadvantaged races, and hence to militarism. It is the most basic form of inequality and deprivation, from which other inequalities of wealth, incomes and resources flow. It deprives people in need of the opportunities of work, food and a livelihood. It leads to waste of resources by neglect, by non-cultivation. It is maintained by unjust immigration laws, leading to illegal immigration and to conflicts.

This apartheid makes people insensitive to the needs of others, to the evils of the past, and does not recognize the human right to the means of livelihood and the responsibility for a just distribution of the earth among all humans. It unconsciously dehumanizes mainly Westerners, both males and females. It is grossly unjust, though legitimized under the prevailing positive international law. Thus the 2000 map of the world according to racial distribution of population to land is roughly the same as in 1900.

Population changes – a challenge to Western conscience

Very significant changes in the distribution of world population have been taking place in the past century and will continue in the coming decades. The population of South Asia (India, Pakistan and Bangladesh) has increased by 900 million since 1945, whereas Australia and Canada still have a combined population of less than 50 million. Details of population projection 1998 to 2025 and land area can be gleaned from *The State of the World Atlas* by Dan Smith.[1] They reveal very clear disparities and imbalances. While the Indian subcontinent, home of India, Pakistan and Bangladesh with 387.3 million hectares of land, will see a population increase of 531 million between 1998 and 2025, the three quasi subcontinents of Australia, Canada, and Russia and Ukraine with together 3,437.1 million hectares of land will experience a population decrease of 9.3 million. The Indian subcontinent is an area of great malnutrition, in which a good number of the 800 million undernourished people of the world live.

The population of China, which increased from 927.8 million in 1975 to 1,255.7 million in 1998, is estimated to be 1,417.7 million by 2015. This means an increase of 327.9 million in 23 years.[2] This growth has been at the human price of compelling this one-fifth of the human race not to have more than one child per family. Between 1975 and 2015 there will be an estimated increase of 489.9 million in China, but the land area of China will remain at 929.1 million hectares. Canada, in contrast, with its 922.1 million hectares, will have an estimated population increase in the next 25 years of only 30 million.

The population of China and the Indian subcontinent will increase by 750 million between 1998 and 2025, while that of Canada, Australia and Russia with Ukraine will decrease by 9.3 million. The Russian land mass of northeast Asia, including Siberia, is an inheritance of colonial expansion by White Russia into Asia.

Inequities in the relationships of population to land will worsen in the coming decades because the ageing populations of the affluent countries are not growing, or not growing so rapidly, as in the poor countries. What is the justice in this situation? Where are the "free economy", "level playing fields" and respect for human rights?

The prevailing laws of immigration and emigration are very racist. They enable the white peoples to migrate and settle in the areas controlled by the Europeans and their descendants. The racially different peoples of Asia and Africa cannot move to the world's underutilized areas. Furthermore, the Western-based TNCs control also a substantial portion of the lands and resources of the poor countries.

There is no reason why European expansionism from 1492 to 1950 should set the pattern of land distribution for the entire future of the human race. Peoples without land should have peaceful, planned access to land without persons. Global human solidarity requires that humanity uses the earth's resources for the common good with a flexible land-population relationship. A world authority should be empowered to bring about a planned and peaceful reallocation of land to peoples. It is one way in which the creative growth of humanity can be related to the use and transformation of the earth.

There should be settlement policies and programmes for moving excess populations to scantily populated areas such as Canada, Australia, the West of the United States, areas of Latin America – in addition to migration within existing national borders. It need not increase pollution and waste, for Third World peoples have long traditions of care for the earth, unlike the present occupants of North America and Australia.

The main barrier, however, would seem to be that these countries – in fact, most countries – do not really consider all human beings equal in rights and dignity. No land-rich country will admit that racism is its basic objection to world population resettlement. All manner of other arguments are alleged, from the point of view of culture to the life-boat theory of triage and survival of the fittest.

Systemic cultural conditioning makes most editors, artists, film producers, universities and educational systems, even international lawyers, ethicists and moral theologians, neglect this world injustice. There must be a deconstruction of the dialogue on communication ethics and international law and justice. Because of cultural conditioning, the just interests of the poor are not taken into account in the public discussion on (communication) ethics, even among the governments of the poor peoples, as in the Non-Aligned Movement.

Some essentials for justice and reconciliation

The example of the grave injustice of land and population indicates the requirements of a global communications ethic. Some demands, made concerning issues such as the excesses of dictators in Latin America and the Holocaust of the Jews under Nazism, may be applied to this issue too. Justice and reconciliation demand that:

1) the truth of what was done to invaded peoples be researched and told publicly, at least to enlighten the present beneficiaries of the source of wealth and power;
2) the memory be preserved of such gross exploitation by European peoples (elites?) during the past 500 years;
3) these findings be officially acknowledged by the present-day beneficiaries of such atrocities;
4) there be punitive justice as in the case of the Nuremberg trials after World War II and Japanese compensation for the Korean "comfort women". Such compensation would be several times more than the so-called debt of the poor countries to the rich ones today.

Thus a Truth Commission and genuine confession, regret and reparation for the damage done may lead to forgiveness and hope of a more just world community.

As Charles Harper writes, "Impunity cries out for redress." It is difficult to expect, however, that the dominant West or the world communications media would accept such an ethic and programme of action concerning the world's greatest injustice. This injustice is usually passed by in silence, a sort of collective amnesia of "developed" humanity. The poor have to accept the world system built by others. Changes at the international level on vital issues such as the land grab by the Western peoples cannot be hoped for even within the foreseeable decades, as the rejection of all such changes is entrenched within the minds of the powerful possessors of invaded lands.

Not reconciling

The communications media hardly help to bring about reconciliation concerning the world's worst genocide, plunder and exploitation of human history, namely, the five centuries of exploitation of the peoples of Asia, Africa and Latin America by Europeans since 1492. Even the Western dominated Christian church media do not deal with this issue. This exploitation is continued through the system of nation-states, foreign debt and the IMF and World Bank Structural Adjustment Programmes imposed on the poor.

The oligopolistic control over communications is a principal obstacle to the reconciliation of peoples. The way of thinking and culture spread by the mass media under neo-liberal globalization is one in which money is the measure of the value of all things. Profit is enthroned as the supreme good for all. Reason itself and human rights are downplayed.

People see and hear much more than before, but it does not mean that they listen attentively to each other. The globalized culture does not make people necessarily wiser and more compassionate to one another. Immense misery exists side by side with enormous wealth and waste. Even though people see much suffering through the TV, in a real sense many are cut off from the misery next door. Or after seeing so much poverty and violence, people become rather indifferent to the suffering of others.

Ensuring a communications ethics with a pluralist worldview is a most difficult mission because of the power of the dominant media magnates. Those who want basic change such as the people's movements for democracy, gender justice, care of the earth and human rights are rather powerless, even in the poor countries. Their means are limited, though Internet and local radio are valuable for resourcing people's struggles. These struggles are generally limited in scope and extent, though significant symbolic mass demonstrations were realized at Seattle in December 1999 and in Prague in September 2000.

A just world order would be one in which:
- every human person is ensured the basic essentials of life and is respected as a person, without discrimination;
- each society is able to provide the basic amenities for the good life of its members and for its cultural development;
- the planet earth is cared for and is so treated that it would be a suitable home for present or future humanity.

For a communications ethics to be just and fair, a world authority is needed to maintain it at the global level. An effective world authority is required to see that the truth is communicated and that falsehood does not prevail in the international media. This is a very difficult task. Since the media cannot be compelled to carry out such a programme, a world authority (such as UNESCO) is required. The New World Information and Communication Order (NWICO) should be organized so as to counter the evils of this global monopoly of communications. Such a move is unlikely, however, for these UN agencies are dependent on the rich countries and super-rich magnates (like Ted Turner) for funds for running their programmes. The super-rich are not likely to be so altruistic as to reduce their wealth or power.

Global education should include presentation of data and history that give the real world situation from the perspectives of different people of the world. Otherwise, the perceptions of the wealthy and the powerful become world news and history. While we may expect individual media personnel to be guided by a communication ethics concerning truth and justice in reporting on personal matters, presently it is not realistic to expect that the world means of communication would function according to an ethic elaborated in terms of world justice. A change or regulation of the ownership of means of communication is a primary reform required for truth and justice in the media, although such a change is not likely in the foreseeable future.

Theoretical norms for communication ethics in a pluralistic worldview may be evolved, but they would not be accepted by the powerful beneficiaries of the prevailing global injustices. For the practical realization of a just world order, there should be a change in the personal values and in the societal structures to respect all human persons regardless of sex, colour, creed, nationality, social function or age.

The best in the Western way of life is democratic and egalitarian; the excesses of capitalism are a deviation from the Western ideal of freedom and justice. The socialist vision of a classless, stateless society is also in the tradition of the apocalyptic vision of the prophets of Judaism. The noblest inspirations of the world's great religions and of secular humanism are in the direction of such a vision. Every major spiritual tradition recognizes that care for others is respect for the sacred in every person, as well as a manifestation of the divine in the caring person.

The pressure of a mass culture of superficiality and social unconcern is bringing about a reaction among the more thoughtful and distressed. The globalization process helps them too to be interconnected in their thinking, exchanging their experiences and networking for desirable changes. Theirs will be a long and difficult struggle, given the power of those entrenched in the dominant world apartheid. The hope of humanity and of nature is in the spread of such positive perspectives of an alternative value system, a social order that respects the human rights of all persons and induces many more persons and groups to act according to their nobler aspirations of loving kindness and sharing. Globalization, shorn of its selfish capitalistic orientation, can thus contain also the hope for a better world order, at the price of much sacrifice by those who opt for it.

A network of common interest

The poor and marginalized risk being fragmented. Realizing the common oppression of the poor everywhere, they should network out of common interest and build viable alternatives. To achieve such unity, they must accept one another, transcending the narrowness of groups, of personality and of identity clashes. Practical wisdom would indicate ways of participation, coming to agreements on goals, priorities, and strategically limiting targets in the short term, while keeping all the groups and issues on-board as long-term objectives.

In this new context, each group must rethink its goals, priorities, means and methods. The choice made decades or centuries earlier may be inadequate to meet present challenges. Some of them may even be counterproductive, such as being within the overall system while advocating piecemeal changes. In the 21st century the leadership is likely to pass to peoples' mass movements based on popularly felt issues. Perhaps some day the people will be convinced that their genuine development, liberation, salvation and happiness can come through other-centred values and life-styles. Then they will freely choose to contest the false gods of capitalism.

International actions against the dominant world powers, TNCs and their products are a strategy with future potential. The global consumers or audience can exercise a healthy influence on the media magnates and TNCs by their choice of media programmes and purchase of goods. The role of peoples' movements throughout the world can be significant, at least in limited struggles.

These orientations require a spirituality of the leaders and of the groups; they must be self-critical, respectful of others' efforts, and mutually supportive in campaigns, along with being willing to make a common evaluation of their efforts. We are all called to transcend our narrow particularities in order to arrive at a higher, wider and deeper level of sharing among all. This call demands a transformation of ourselves from within our innermost being, to accept all others as sisters and brothers. Our growth to a planetary dimension is an invitation to spiritual deepening, a purification from selfishness to a more universal communion in real life, to our own humanization. In so far as we do so, we shall become more truly civilized, approach the ideals of the best in all our religions and cultures, and pursue the deepest and best aspirations of every human heart and mind.

NOTES

[1] London, Penguin, 1999, pp.104-11.
[2] UN Development Programme, *Human Development Report 2000*, London, Oxford UP, 2000.

Who Are We? Restoring the Language, Cultural Memory and Identity of Estonia

EPP LAUK

Once in my student years in the 1970s, when I was on my way to the university city of Tartu, an elderly man sitting next to me in the bus suddenly asked: "Why do you Estonians hate Russians?"

My spontaneous answer was: "We don't hate Russians."

"But you don't like them either. Why?" the man continued.

In the following conversation (in Russian), I learned that the man was a retired military pilot in Tartu, where one of the biggest military airports of the former Soviet Union was situated. With pride in his voice he told me that he considered himself a native of Tartu, as he had bombed the city during the Red Army offensives in 1944 and had lived there since 1952. I immediately remembered the photographs I had seen at home of my mother and father clearing the city of ruins right after the war, while they were students in Tartu. It was a shocking experience to talk to someone who was proud to be responsible for the damage.

When I then switched to Estonian, expecting that he certainly knew the language since he regarded himself as a native, the man smiled in a friendly way and said, "Please speak human language. I do not understand Estonian, except for a few words."

We live in a multiethnic and multiracial world. Every attempt to change it means sacrificing the lives of millions of innocent people, as the past and present of humankind clearly proves. Herder's concept that all nations are equally valuable – *Denn jedes Volk ist Volk; es hat seine National Bildung wie seine Sprache* (Every people is a people; they have their own national culture, just as they have their own language) – is even more significant today than it was in the 18th century. Every nation tries to maintain and protect the basic conditions that make it a nation: the language, indigenous culture, traditions, territory, religion. These are also the existential needs of human beings – to belong somewhere, to have an identity that helps to interpret and understand the surrounding social reality. Identity represents an important part of individual and collective self-consciousness that is created in social interaction. It can be changed, destroyed and reconstructed. Identity is also essential in order to be able to tolerate "others" who are different from "us".

During great political upheavals and crises, people most often face the need to define or redefine their national, cultural, political and other identities. During the last decade, the world saw the collapse of an entire political system – socialism in central Europe and the former Soviet Union. Building up civic society, democratic institutions, a new political culture and market economy is a complicated process that contains a lot of controversies, both hidden and open conflicts, which different groups in society perceive and interpret differently. Success in this process largely depends on how the nations in transition answer the questions: Who are we? Where do we come from? Where are we going? They ask such questions in order to come to terms with their past, overcome conflicts and create a positive future for their new generations. In deeply altered circumstances, people need to think about themselves and to relate to others in profoundly new ways.

After the fall of the Berlin Wall, nations of the former "socialist bloc" gradually freed themselves from identities imposed by the regime and started to restore their old historical identities and search for new ones. It was important for those formerly oppressed nations to reassert themselves in order to cope with the historical injustice they suffered. This process has been accompanied by tensions and conflicts that are largely ethnic and that have even taken the form of massacres and genocide in some regions (e.g. former Yugoslavia), or a less gory form of hatred and xenophobia in others.

The most complicated burden of the Soviet legacy – the "Russian issue" – became a major challenge for the young Estonian democracy after the restoration of the independent nation-state. In Estonia the immigrant community is many times larger than in any other European country today. For both the indigenous and immigrant population, political and social changes raised the issue of redefining their identities to find non-violent, constructive solutions to the problems facing both communities. Reconciliation on both collective and individual bases has become an important issue of recovering from a difficult past and looking ahead to the future. This process involves an ongoing interplay of ethical communication, identity and membership. Concerning Estonia today, membership is being challenged from within and without – from within by Estonians and their dramatic political past, and by Russophones facing the need to relate to Estonia and Estonians in a new way; from without by the European Union (EU) and, as before, by the Russian state.

Why is history important?

Up to 1940 Estonia was almost a monoethnic country, with the Estonian population then at 88.2 percent, Russians 8.2 percent and the other ethnic groups 3.6 percent. During 50 years of Soviet rule, the share of Estonians among a population of about 1.5 million decreased to 61.5 percent, the share of Russians increased to 30.3 percent and the other nations to 8.2 percent by 1989. By then people of 121 ethnic origins considered Estonia their home country. They had very different mentalities, cultural backgrounds and traditions. An important distinctive feature that unites this population is their common language – Russian. They therefore are also called Russophones. During the Soviet period, Russian was the only language of education for these people in Estonia.

The way this large Russophone community historically emerged largely explains the complicated nature of interethnic relations and the difficulties confronting the social and political integration of Russians in Estonian society today. Immigrants were not welcomed in Estonia because they were used as the tools of occupation and colonization by the Soviet totalitarian regime. Most of the people who settled in Estonia after 1945, however, had barely any idea of what had happened to the country. An Orwellian Ministry of Truth was busy compiling the "Soviet history" of Estonia, claiming that the mass deportations in 1941 and 1949 were aimed at the "liquidation of enemies of the nation and socialism" and not the destruction of the lives of over 30,000 Estonians, mostly women and children. Their empty homes were soon resettled by Russian-speaking newcomers.

The industrial cities in northeastern Estonia that were destroyed in the war were rebuilt and repopulated by people of mostly Russian origin during the post-war decades. Until the late 1950s, the authorities even forbade Estonians to resettle in Narva, an Estonian-Russian border city. As a result, around 80-90 percent of the population of the northeastern Estonian cities speak Russian. Almost half of the inhabitants of the capital, Tallinn, are Russophones.[1]

The Soviet colonization policy was strengthened with the myth of the Soviet Union as a common homeland for all the *Soviet* people. According to this myth, the Soviet people were a homogeneous group. Huge efforts were made to create citizens loyal to the USSR with no other competing identity. According to this ideology, a Soviet citizen was at home everywhere in a territory covering more than one-sixth of the earth. The common language of international communication for all "Soviet peoples" was naturally the most widely used one – Russian. "My address is neither a house nor a street, my address is the Soviet Union" was a popular song that preached exactly this myth. In 1986, fully 78 percent of Russians in Estonia identified themselves as "Soviets".

In addition, in the "Soviet republics" Russophones enjoyed certain privileges that were not available to the indigenous people. They had better possibilities to get well-paid jobs, especially in the spheres of industry and services. Large so-called all-Soviet strategic industrial enterprises in Estonia employed exclusively immigrant workers. In the cities they were provided with new flats immediately upon arrival, while Estonians had few chances to improve their living conditions. Large new districts were built up for immigrant people in all big cities. They felt comfortable speaking only Russian and never had a serious need to socialize with the indigenous Estonian population.

Social injustice created a potential source of conflicts in everyday life and provoked national hatred on an individual basis. Certain spheres of life were especially sensitive, for example medical services and communal transport. In many cities in the 1980s, more and more doctors were employed who had no knowledge of Estonian whatsoever. They were mostly family members of Soviet Army officers. They could be good specialists, but they were not required to learn Estonian. As the system did not allow a patient to choose a doctor, Estonians who were not able to describe their health problems in Russian (usually children and elderly people) did not receive qualified help. An Estonian was usually willing to communicate with his or her Russian neighbours without prejudice. However, when help for a sick child could not be obtained because of the ignorance of a doctor who could not be bothered to learn a word of Estonian, feelings of anger simultaneously provoked national hatred against Russians.

Furthermore, the Soviet migration policy was accompanied by Russification, which achieved its peak in the late 1970s with the forcible imposition of the Russian language in every sphere of life in Estonia. By that time, Russian was already used as a dominant language in official settings as well as in many spheres of everyday life, including public transport, banks, shops and post offices. Competence in Russian among Estonians was improving and encouraged in all possible ways: teaching it in kindergartens, increasing the number of lessons in Russian at the cost of Estonian in Estonian schools and so forth. A special journal called *Russian Language in Estonian Schools* was established. At the same time, the Estonian language in Russian schools was taught as an optional subject, if at all.

From 1976 all academic theses submitted in "Soviet republics" had to be written in Russian, even if they were about the Estonian language, literature or folklore. As a result of Russification, by the early 1980s Estonians had a much worse linguistic position in their home country than Russophones did. According to a survey carried out in 1990, of all Russians in Estonia 65 percent reported that they did not have problems with communicating exclusively in Russian, and 21 percent reacted positively to the statement "It is senseless to start learning Estonian".[2] In contrast, Estonians had acquired sufficient knowledge of Russian to be able to communicate with local Russians and with the authorities.

The colonization policy together with Russification thus encouraged the Russophone population to develop their Russian based Soviet identity. This self-consciousness excluded interest in indigenous Estonian culture and cultivated a superficial and ignorant attitude towards "aborigines". Official policy, on the one hand, and the specific significance of mother tongue for Estonians' self-perception and national self-esteem, on the other, built up distinct language barriers between the two main ethnic communities. As a consequence, it was very difficult for Russophone people to adjust to the changed linguistic situation after the restoration of the Estonian nation-state.

On the individual level, two attitudes developed towards Russians. On the one hand, as representatives of the Soviet regime, in people's minds they were associated with crimes and injustices carried out by the regime. "Russian" became the synonym of "enemy". On the other hand, it was important to judge how a person who spoke Russian and came to live and work in Estonia was related to the political regime. Where the distinction could be made, the reconciliation was much easier. Not everybody was seen as occupier, enemy or unbidden guest. When for example, in the 1950s, several Russian-speaking Jewish scholars from Russia settled in Tartu to escape persecution, they were welcomed into Tartu University. They learned to communicate in Estonian very soon, and Estonians did not consider them intruders.

Resistance to Russification

The Russification policy, successful in some nations like Belarus or Kazakhstan, met rather strong resistance in all the Baltic countries. This resistance in Estonia and Latvia took the form of covert opposition, based on ethnic and cultural values like mother tongue, national symbols and historical memory of the nation, and it was expressed in the cultural public sphere. In Lithuania the Catholic Church and religion also played an important role.

A certain manifestation of solidarity and resistance among the Baltic nations appeared in the way they used Russian as the "language of international communication". Russian was the only alternative for an Estonian, Latvian and Lithuanian to be able to understand each other at that time. Knowledge of other foreign languages was not sufficient, and they also generally had a very poor knowledge of each others' languages. To demonstrate that "I am not Russian although I am speaking Russian to you", they would intentionally use a broken form of Russian as a lingua franca.

The continuously decreasing Estonian population and the increasing numbers of Russophone immigrants, together with aggressive Russification. were clear threats to Estonian national existence. In 1980 some 40 well-known intellectuals (scientists, writers, journalists and artists) wrote a letter to the Soviet authorities and the press in which they expressed their concerns about the situation. They clearly defined the reasons for growing tension between the two main ethnic groups. They indicated the uncertainty and fear of losing national identity among Estonians, the difficulties facing the non-Estonian population in strengthening their identity, and the lack of confidence and mutual understanding between the two communities. They stressed that, historically, the mother tongue had always been for Estonians a symbol of human dignity, and therefore "A person who lives in Estonia for years and does not respect Estonian language and culture, deeply offends – intentionally or not, consciously or not – the human dignity of Estonian people. Attitude towards the Estonian language is a key question in the formation of relations between Estonians and other nationalities in Estonia." The letter was never published in the newspapers. The only response from the authorities was the persecution of those who signed the letter.

Identity as a means of national survival

In the construction of national identities, sovereignty forms an important discursive element. In a broader sense, through sovereignty, nationalist discourse imagines the world as a system of nations separated from each other by exclusive borders. These borders form a symbol of nation and national identity and divide the world into "them" and "us".[3] Sovereignty is defined in terms of otherness. In this sense, sovereignty can also be used as a means of constructing invisible barriers to protect national identity. In many cases, especially in Eastern Europe, language and history have been used to define the nation and to build borders against dangerous otherness. As Benedict Anderson demonstrates, the national spirit could often be seen in the language of a nation and in its culture expressed through language.[4]

This analysis applies to Estonia. Language, cultural traditions and history have been the three most important "bricks" of nation-building and have served as a means of national survival under various foreign oppressors. The Estonian language became a crucial national attribute for Estonians, the symbol of human dignity, a value that united people since Estonians began to consolidate on an ethnic basis and develop as a nation in the middle of the 19th century. National development was tightly bound up with language-based cultural development. There was no Estonian national architecture or fine arts in the 19th century, but there was a national literature, an epic folklore and linguistic studies, a periodical press and very popular choral music traditions.

Naturally, education was an important factor in the development of national culture. The rate of literacy among Estonian people, already about 60 percent by the end of the 18th century, approached 95 percent according to the census data of 1897. A leader of the Estonian national movement, Jakob Hurt, defined the way of national survival in 1869 as follows: "A small nation like the Estonians can never become great in number and powerful politically, but even the smallest nation can become mighty spiritually and intellectually." Thus, as the Estonian ethnic territory was not yet an administrative unit but a part of the Russian Baltic provinces, national identity was historically shaped mainly in linguistic and cultural terms.

The historical dimension of national identity was also created in the 19th century. The main idea was the myth of a "golden age" of freedom before the German conquest in the early 13th century. In the imagined distant national past, this age had been the only period of freedom for Estonians up to the establishment of the independent state in 1918. This independence lasted barely 20 years, but it became a part of the myth of the "golden age" for the decades under Soviet occupation. Historical experience of the cultural resistance against the Germanification and Russification in the 19th century contributed to the ability of the nation to hide behind cultural and language barriers under the later Soviet occupation. Historical memory constituted an essential aspect in supporting national feelings and became a part of national identity.[5] Attempts to destroy it had the opposite effect.

The Soviet authorities fully recognized the menace to Soviet ideology of the existence of 20 years of "Estonian time" in the nation's memory. Therefore an official version of the history of these years and of the Soviet annexation in 1940 was fabricated. Everything that could be a reminder of lost independence was destroyed (e.g. millions of copies of books and periodicals published between 1918 and 1940). Names of public figures, authors, artists and others were cut out from encyclopaedias, lists of forbidden literature and names of people were compiled and similar steps were taken.

This highly controlled official history was certainly very effective in shaping what immigrant people knew and believed about Estonia's past, but it was not so effective among Estonians themselves. The Russophone media amplified the official history, conveying the thought that the only choice for Estonia was, is and would be development within the USSR. As surveys show, about one-third of Russophone people still believe that independent Estonia was a bourgeois, authoritarian regime with features of fascism; that the incorporation of Estonia into the Soviet Union in 1940 was by the will of Estonian people; and that the Soviet years were a period of positive development.[6]

In contrast, quite powerful, quasi-institutionalized forms of "unofficial" history existed that made resistance to the official versions possible. In his book *Mind as Action* (1998), James Wertsch demonstrates the ways in which Estonians developed their "unofficial" history interpretations and how they used them to avoid the Soviet version of Estonia's history. "Even in school, a context where teachers and students had to be vigilant about maintaining a façade of loyalty to the USSR, there were ways for teachers to encourage students to develop tactics of resistance.... Instruction about official history was often accompanied by clear indications from teachers that what they were teaching was not to be believed." Estonians "made a clear distinction between knowing an official history and not believing it, on the one hand, and knowing and believing an unofficial history, on the other".[7]

As surveys prove, the immigrant population did not have such historical consciousness as a part of their identity.[8] Different interpretations and understandings of history were thus one of the sources that created misunderstanding and mistrust between the two main ethnic groups in Estonia. A radical reappraisal of the official history and breakdown of the Soviet myths in the early 1990s was a bigger shock for non-Estonians than for Estonians. Estonians saw it as a restoration of justice – the crimes committed by the Soviet regime and its stooges were finally publicly revealed. Something that was never allowed to be mentioned was clearly articulated. Non-Estonians were confused; their positive history interpretation was destroyed, and they asked, What is the truth?

As noted, language and literature played a crucial role in supporting national identity and at opposing the official ideology and policy. This resistance developed into forms of "double thinking", metaphoric language, writing and reading "between the lines" or "behind the lines" that spread widely, especially from the 1960s. Authors and journalists became ingenious at such "language games", and readers were equally astute in discovering the hidden messages.[9] When the censorship authorities discovered the "tricks" after publication, the authors were punished. This practice, however, supported feelings of national dignity and indicated to the people that it was still possible to find a sanctuary from oppressive forces. Not many believed they would see the demise of those forces, although most people kept their hopes alive.

One typical example comes from 1980, when an art student published a poem in the literary magazine *Looming* (Creature). The poem was a masterly description of a picture that a young man saw before his eyes standing at the seaside. Taking the first letters of each line, however, a reader could put together the word *sinimustvalge* (blue-black-white), the combination of colours symbolizing independence, the colours of the flag of the Estonian Republic. It was absolutely forbidden to use these colours together in public texts or images. As a result, the student was expelled from the university on the grounds of improper behaviour for a Soviet student.

The discourse of passive resistance was especially widespread in the private sphere. Usually young people heard unofficial versions of history within their family circles. The generation of the 1920s had experienced the pre-war independent Estonia, participating in the war on one side of the front or the other (while neither of them was "ours") and the post-war Soviet occupation. Along with real facts young people also learned about the pain and anger that accompanied these experiences. Sometimes they were turned into family secrets that were not told to children to protect them and the family from persecution by the authorities. It was better not to know than to keep a secret. I was already 16 years old when I first heard that my father had fought in the war "on the wrong side". When the KGB discovered this fact, he lost his position as vice-rector of an agricultural school and was persecuted by the KGB for years thereafter. The other son of the same family, my uncle, had fought on the "right side" and enjoyed the privileges of a "veteran of the Great Patriotic War".

This family difference had not been their deliberate choice, but two alien superpowers had put them in the position of enemies. They did not become enemies within the family, however, although one was socially privileged and the other had to disavow his past to retain a minimum of safety. The fact that neither brother was a voluntary supporter of these superpowers made reconciliation in the family possible.

The same argument applies to society: it was the totalitarian regime that placed different ethnic and social groups in confrontation and made them responsible for the consequences. The collapse of the oppressing regime created new grounds for genuine reconciliation in Estonia. People of various nationalities and backgrounds who consider Estonia their home must overcome the heritage of the past and adapt to living together within the framework of a newly reborn nation-state. This task presupposes that new identities, adequate to these changed circumstances, will be built up. This is not an easy and fast process. It brings various difficulties and complications, but it is still possible, as the experience of Estonia demonstrates.

Given the historical, political and cultural conditions described above, the two communities, Estonian and Russophone, coexisted in the same territory but communicated with each other only in spheres where it was unavoidable. The prejudices, ignorance and misunderstandings that emerged and gradually grew because of lack of adequate information about each other also fed the fears of both parties after the new independence. This situation was immediately used by those generating propaganda hostile to Estonia's independence, inspiring the Russophone population to think that they would become a second-class people in the Estonian Republic, that Estonians would deport them to Russia and leave them without jobs, homes and education.

New independence and two communities

Independence indeed had different meanings and importance for the two ethnic communities. Estonians felt they had reacquired their "golden age". They started to rebuild their national state as a legal successor to the Republic of Estonia of the 1920s and 1930s. During the early 1990s the Constitution, Language Law, Citizens' Law, Aliens' Law, Law of the Cultural Autonomy of Minorities and other new laws that directly influenced the status of the non-ethnic Estonian population were adopted, and the Estonian currency *kroon* was introduced.

New independence and democracy (although certainly rather insufficient in many respects) gave Estonians the feeling of becoming masters in their own house, and the conviction that they too are the subjects of human rights. Along with the end of political and cultural oppression, the fear of becoming a minority in their native country disappeared. New difficulties, connected with the building up of a civic society, democratic institutions and market economy were similar for all inhabitants of Estonia.

For the Russophone community, the same events had a different meaning. Re-establishment of the Estonian nation-state left most of them without citizenship, as they were not automatically granted Estonian citizenship. They became occupiers, immigrants, illegal residents, a minority in the country where they had been at home for years and decades or all their lives. They faced uncertainty, fear and insecurity; the situation appeared unfair and offensive. Who are we? What is going to happen to us? Where do we belong? were frequent questions among the Russophone people and in public discussion. Their former identity as citizens of the USSR was destroyed, and nothing automatically compensated for this loss. According to new Estonian laws, only about 80,000 non-Estonians acquired Estonian citizenship by birth, while the remaining 400,000 had to apply for naturalization or for residency permits. The demand that every applicant for citizenship had to pass a spoken and written Estonian language examination caused strong protests, especially among the older generation, who claimed not to be able to learn

Estonian. In the Russian media and Russia's propaganda abroad, the language issue in Estonia (and similarly in Latvia) was presented as a violation of human rights.

Concerning citizenship, Russians and Russophones of other nationalities had different options. People originating from former "Soviet republics" or "socialist nations" like Lithuanians, Armenians, Ukrainians and Hungarians could, among other choices, apply for citizenship of the country of their origin, and many did so.

"Mother Russia", however, which Russians had consciously or subconsciously always relied on, did not recognize them as her children or grant them Russian citizenship. Moreover, they were used in Russia's political interests. The "near abroad" (the territories close to the borders of Russia) faced demands automatically to grant these Russians citizenship of the state of residence and to give Russian the status of second official language. The covert idea of these demands was that Russians would never have to learn the other official language. They could manage in Russian just like before, and Russian would have remained the dominant language in the public sphere.

Small nations with a young democracy like Estonia and Latvia, which have enclaves of their larger neighbours in their territory, are vulnerable to their neighbours' political and cultural expansionism, and therefore the immigrant population is considered a source of constant insecurity. Surveys made in Estonia during the 1990s confirm this point. Although the general state of interethnic relations is evaluated by both Russians and Estonians as positive and improving, Estonians expressed mistrust about Russian politics and Russians' potential behaviour in the future. Only one third of respondents were convinced of the loyalty of Russians to Estonia, whereas 65 percent were of the opinion that Russians were not loyal and were dreaming of restoring the Soviet empire.[10] The Citizenship Law, adopted in 1995, seems to have served here as a certain guarantee of Estonian identity.

A striking fact is that according to the above mentioned study, mistrust between the two main ethnic groups is asymmetrical: Russians do not perceive Russia or themselves as a real threat to Estonians. This result points to another fact that has also been proved by social scientists, namely, that the reputation of Russia is declining among Estonian Russians and other Russophones, and their loyalty towards Russia, especially among younger generations, is gradually weakening.[11] This finding also indicates what a decisive role Estonian policy has in choosing paths to develop the future identity of the Russophone minority.

Among the positive factors that shape a new group identity for Russophones is their rather strong territorial identity with Estonia. Russians identify themselves territorially and culturally as "Estonian Russians", and among the younger generations, as "native Russians of Estonia". For a remarkably large part of them, "Baltic Russians" has a meaning.[12] The identity of Russophones has been constructed on the idea that the state determines the nation, but Estonian identity is constructed on the principle that a nation is entitled to seek its own state.[13]

Within the framework of the nation-state, an essential pre-condition to cross-cultural borders between the Estonian majority and the non-Estonian minority is the Russophones' readiness to learn the Estonian language. Social practice, the educational system amd the decades-long tradition of the two communities living by themselves and communicating mainly in Russian obstruct this readiness. In connection with the political changes in Estonian society, however, the value of Estonian as a means of better adjustment to the new conditions is widely recognized. According to a survey, the proportion of Russophones who agreed that one cannot get by in Estonia without knowing the Estonian language increased from 30 percent in 1990 to 82 percent in 1995. Over 50 percent of Russian parents who themselves do not speak Estonian agreed that their children must know Estonian.[14] To a certain extent this trend has strengthened the motivation to learn Estonian, as young people understand that knowledge of Estonian provides them with better prospects for getting higher education and good jobs. There is a growing tendency among Russophone families to educate their children in Estonian schools. A significant increase of competence in the Estonian language among the Russophone population, however, is likely to be a long-term process. Only 20 percent of people between the ages of 15 and 40 actively use Estonian in their everyday communication with Estonians.[15]

As there seems to be relatively little chance of Russophones constructing a new type of ethnic cultural identity of their own, it is possible that non-ethnic identities and a new global cultural orientation will shape their new group identity. Among young generations of Russophones, the search for a European identity seems to be growing.[16] Local territorial self-identification will probably help Russophones to develop loyalty towards the Estonian state in the broader context of a federal Europe. Another non-ethnic identity resource for Russians in Estonia seems to be the growing importance of the Orthodox Church. While Estonians are mostly Lutherans, the Orthodox faith has become a unifying value for the Russophone community as a symbol of their common cultural identity.

The most important factor during the past decade that has helped to stabilize interethnic relations in Estonia has been economic development. The problems inevitably accompanying a transition to a market economy were understood by both communities.[17] Liberal economic reforms contributed to the fact that even at the tensest moment in ethnic relations during 1991-93, the problems did not result in outbursts of violence and conflict.

Moreover, attitudes between the two ethnic groups are considered to be improving in general. Both groups seem to sense what troubles the other party with regard to each other. Although differences in ethnic character are recognized as a problem that complicates mutual understanding and everyday communication, they do not create hatred on an ethnic basis.[18] Dissatisfaction within national discourse, rather, focuses on the state bureaucracy and the difficulties connected with obtaining Estonian citizenship. This tone is reflected also in the Russophone press, which makes a clear distinction between the Estonian state and its people, and makes state policy and bureaucracy responsible for the problems of the minority population. Furthermore, compared to the early 1990s, the general attitude of the Russophone media towards Estonia's national policy has become more tolerant. The Russophone media have also expressed a hope that the integration of Estonia into the European Union will contribute to improving relations between the state and the Russophone minority by easing some conditions of obtaining citizenship and residence permits.[19]

The development of Estonian society and its economy after independence has fostered the search for a new group identity among the Russophone minority. It has seen that safe and stable integration and reconciliation are possible if it accepts the rules constitutionally established by the newly formed home-state. These rules do not restrict the cultural diversity of minorities but are aimed at safeguarding the cultural identity of the native population. A special Law on the Cultural Autonomy of Minorities has even been passed to protect non-Estonians' cultural development within the Estonian nation-state.

National identity and globalization

How do people in Estonia reconcile themselves to the omnipresence of the English language and Americanized values reflected in the globalization of culture during recent times, especially via the media? Is there a fear that indigenous language and culture that had such an important role in rescuing national identity and dignity under the Soviet oppression will ultimately be diminished and damaged?

Apart from its positive features, globalization certainly has negative aspects for the cultural development of Estonia. There really is no comparison, however, between the USSR's language and national policy and the mechanism of globalization. Russification was an official policy aimed at promoting Russian at the cost of restricted use of Estonian. Russification was also forcible, with distinct political pressures behind it. The spread of English is not a danger to the existence of the nation. Moreover, it is connected with the notion of progress for the peoples of eastern Europe. Communication with the rest of the world takes place mostly in English, and it is the language of the Internet, a significant channel for globalization. Knowledge of English helps in getting a better education, earning money, travelling and so forth. Learning and using English is voluntary. Nobody forces one to speak English, and its spread is not aggressive as Russification was.

English is also a means to communicate with the larger world about ourselves. We are understood. We can use it to present our own views of ourselves. We could not do the same with Russian, despite the Soviet claim that Russian was a world language. People are interested in learning English (as well as other foreign languages), and it has become very popular in Estonia. Demand for teachers of English has increased incredibly, as well as the quality of teaching. English is popular also among Russophone people for the same reasons. They learn English even more willingly than they learn Estonian. Estonian helps them to manage better at home, English enables them to be successful around the world.

Estonia is now considering joining the EU. Does not such a step represent the danger of reversing all the gains in reconciliation achieved by people from different ethnic and social backgrounds in Estonia? Will it not reignite the fears and hatreds that have riven the Baltic states and, by implication, many other societies in Europe? Evidence and experience suggest the contrary.

The restoration of the Estonian nation-state made people from the Russian and the Estonian communities more aware of their political, cultural and ethnic differences. Whereas these differences initially threatened to create more tension between the groups, changing political and personal attitudes supported by economic, legal and social reforms seem to have made possible a gradual increase in mutual confidence. The two "parallel" communities have turned their faces towards each other and entered into dialogue. Looking at it from an optimistic viewpoint, the development of such confidence may be seen as one decisive factor in the cultural and political integration of the Russophone population in Estonia, which is searching for its own particular identity within the Estonian state. The ability of the Estonian nation to initiate and pursue the process of reconciliation and integration is an indication that there is little fear of its identity being lost in an enlarged EU. That Estonia has

this confidence suggests that reconciliation will continue and that the
rest of the world can learn much from the process.

NOTES

[1] See http://stat.vil.ee/pks/rahvus/est/index.html.
[2] T. Vihalemm and L. Lauristin, "Cultural Adjustment to the Changing Societal Environment: The
Case of Russians in Estonia", in *Return to the Western World: Cultural and Political Perspectives in the Estonian Post-Communist Transition*, ed. Marju Lauristin and Peeter Vihalemm, with
Karl Erik Rosengren and Lennart Weibull, Tartu, Tartu UP, 1997, pp.279-98.
[3] M. Lehti, "Sovereignty, Borders and the Construction of National Identities in Estonia and Latvia", in *The Dividing Line: Borders and National Peripheries*, ed. Lars-Folke Landgren and
Manun Häyrynen, Helsinki, Univ. of Helsinki, 1997, p.43.
[4] B. Anderson, *Imagined Communities: Reflections on the Origin and Spread of Nationalism*,
London, VERSO, 1996.
[5] R. Ruutsoo, "Eesti ja vene koolide õpilaste ajalooteadvus 1992-1993" (Historical consciousness
of the students in Estonian and Russian schools in 1992-1993), in *Vene noored Eestis: Sotsio-
loogilinie mosaiik* (Russian youth in Estonia: A sociological mosaic), ed. P. Järve, Tartu, Tartu
UP, 1997, pp.83-92; A. Valk, "Venelaste ja eestlaste ajaloolisest identiteedist" (On the historical
identity of Russians and Estonians), in *ibid.*, pp.93-97.
[6] Ruutsoo, "Eesti".
[7] J.V. Wertsch, *Mind as Action*, New York, Oxford UP, 1998, pp.153-54,158.
[8] Valk, "Venelaste"; Ruutsoo, "Eesti".
[9] See S. Hoyer, E. Lauk and P. Vihalemm, eds, *Towards a Civic Society: The Baltic Media's Long
Road to Freedom. Perspectives on History, Ethnicity and Journalism*, Tartu, Baltic Association
for Media Research/Nota Batlica Ltd, 1993.
[10] A. Kirch, M. Kirch and T. Tuisk, "Vene noorte etnilise ja kultuurilise identiteedi muutused aas-
tatel 1993-1996" (Changes in the ethnic and cultural identities of the Russian youth in 1993-
1996), in *Vene noored Eestis*, ed. Järve, pp.47-68.
[11] T. Vihalemm, *Formation of Collective Identity among Russophone Population of Estonia*, Tartu,
Tartu UP, 1999.
[12] Vihalemm and Lauristin, "Cultural Adjustment".
[13] Vihalemm, *Formation*.
[14] Vihalemm and Lauristin, "Cultural Adjustment".
[15] Vihalemm, *Formation*.
[16] Kirch, Kirch and Tuisk, "Vene".
[17] Vihalemm and Lauristin, "Cultural Adjustment".
[18] J. Kruusvll, "Rahvusprobleemid rahva pilgu läbi 1996" (Ethnic problems through the eyes of
people in 1996), in *Vene noored Eestis*, ed. Järve, pp.131-49; idem, "Usaldus ja usaldamatus rah-
vussuhetes" (Trust and distrust in ethnic relations), in *Vene küsimus ja Eesti valikud* (The Russian issue and Estonia's choices), ed. Mati Heidmets, Tallinn, TPU Press, 1998, pp.29-76.
[19] V. Jakobson, "Constructing National Identity by the Russophone Press in Estonia in 1947-1996",
paper presented at the third Nordic-Baltic Summer School on the Media and Communication
Studies, Ventspils, 2000.

The Spirit of Community:
First Nations Peoples and Canadian Society

BERNIE HARDER AND MARLENE CUTHBERT

Canada's biggest challenge in the 21st century is to achieve harmony with the Native, or First Nations, people, whose land the country occupies.[1] The Declaration of First Nations Chiefs and Elders below summarizes central themes on which First Nations people build communities.

> We the original peoples of the land know the Creator put us here.
> The Creator gave us laws that govern all our relationships to live in harmony with nature and mankind.
> The laws of the Creator defined our rights and responsibilities.
> The Creator gave us our spiritual beliefs, our languages, our culture, and a place on Mother Earth who provided us with all our needs.
> We have maintained our freedom, our languages, and our traditions from time immemorial.
> We continue to exercise the rights and fulfil the responsibilities and obligations given to us by the Creator for the land upon which we are placed.
> The Creator has given us the right to govern ourselves and the right to self determination.
> The rights and responsibilities given to us by the Creator cannot be altered or taken away by any other nation.[2]

Community is based on spirit – the Creator – and is fundamentally related to the land. First Nations author Kateri Akiwenzie-Damm writes:

> We belong to this land. The land does not belong to us.... Land, community, culture and spirituality are intricately woven together.... Who you are as an Indigenous person arises from your connection to the land and to all others who share it. Your community thus includes everything that is connected to the land: the human, the natural and the supernatural.... It is about love, and respect, honesty and truth. So we say truly that the land is our mother, Mother Earth.... As Indigenous people of this land, our view of the world and our daily experience differs significantly from that of other people in Canada, of Canadians.[3]

Aboriginal cultures could teach us a great deal about the spirit of community. This chapter draws on some of those teachings to explore ways in which Aboriginal and non-Aboriginal people in Canada can enhance the spirit of community both within and between them, with a view to building bridges that respect difference. First Nations people have told us that this community-building would include:

1) people in each community getting together to discuss what to do;
2) all sides beginning with spirituality;
3) each community following the best of its own spiritual teachings and acting out of its humanity;
4) careful listening with a commitment to responding with action, not just "understanding" and words.

Literature can express much about the spirit of a people, and the first part of this chapter draws on selected Aboriginal authors in Canada. Since colonialism in Canada causes much disintegration of Native communities, Aboriginal literature often focuses on healing broken communities, both within Aboriginal culture and between Aboriginal and non-Aboriginal cultures.

The second part of the chapter provides concrete examples of attempts to heal communities in the 21st century. We examine the values underlying successful peace-making within Aboriginal communities achieved by using traditional "sentencing circles". We also examine the attempts at bridge-building between Aboriginal and non-Aboriginal communities as major denominations in Canada try to overcome the devastation that more than a century of residential schools caused for Native communities.

The voices of First Nations authors

In 1847 George Copway, an Ojibwa Methodist minister, became the first Canadian Indian to publish a book in English.[4] One of his main concerns was to explain the Ojibwa way of life and the tribe's struggle against degradation. He opposes the stereotypes that were being promoted at the time and also argues for the actions needed to rescue his people from the desperate effects of colonization. Unfortunately, he also promotes some of the stereotypes, demonstrating how powerful internalized colonization can be. Since then, Native authors have continued to use their gifts to create a large corpus of outstanding literary works and at the same time to seek for healing and just solutions.

Emily Pauline Johnson (Mohawk, 1861-1913) combined the oral tradition of her people and the written legacy of British literature to become an internationally acclaimed voice and author. Her work includes harsh criticism of colonial injustice as well as celebration. In her words: "My aim, my joy, my pride is to sing the glories of my people."[5] Her powerful poem "The Cattle Thief", written in defence of Eagle Chief, who was ruthlessly shot by the settlers for "stealing" a cow, ends with the defiant words of his daughter proclaiming the evils of settlers and a programme for change:

What have you left to us of land, what have you left of game,
What have you brought but evil, and curses since you came?

. . . .

Give back the furs and the forests that were ours before you came;
Give back the peace and the plenty. Then come with your new belief,
And blame, if you dare, the hunger that *drove* him to be a thief.[6]

These demands find an echo in contemporary First Nations communities, in people like Willie Boisseneau of Garden River First Nation: "All we want is that the Canadian government and society pay us the actual debts they owe us."[7] The Native Peoples in Canada have been denied even what is clearly owed them, as is made very clear by the 1991 *Report of the Aboriginal Justice Inquiry of Manitoba*. Based on a detailed examination of the legalities in the province of Manitoba, it states that "there should be no controversy today surrounding the issue of treaty land entitlements.... Under the numbered treaties, the Indian nations of Manitoba were promised explicitly by the Crown that they would retain large tracts of land for their permanent and exclusive use." In Manitoba alone, the report states, the outstanding treaty land entitlement exceeds a million acres of Crown land.[8] This is just a beginning of what Canada owes First Nations peoples.

Armand Garnet Ruffo, Ojibwa author and professor at Carleton University in Ottawa, comments that a focus on community is common to Native authors who write as individuals but, more significantly, as part of a community:

> As an expression of voice, or, more correctly, a community of voices, Native writers are attempting to find expression in a society that does not share their values and concerns. The form of these voices, like content itself, varies according to individual author, but as community, theirs is a collective voice that addresses the relationship between colonizer and colonized, the impact of colonialism, and, moreover, functions on a practical level by striving to bring about positive change. Thus, my claim is that Native literature, while grounded in a traditional, spiritually based worldview, is no less a call for liberation, survival, and beyond to affirmation.[9]

Ruffo's views are supported by C. Murray Sinclair, a First Nations associate chief judge in Manitoba, in an article explaining the systemic reasons for suicide by Native people:

> We can no longer restrict ourselves to writings intended only to educate white people about who we are. We need that type of writing, but we need more. We need Aboriginal people to write about twentieth-century Aboriginality; about what it means and where it is going and, most important, about where it should be going. As Aboriginal people we need to begin to think about issues that we would have been thinking about if we had control of our lives at this point.[10]

A few examples from the literature of other Native authors will illustrate this frequently repeated vision. Dr Arthur Solomon, an Anishinabe elder, is respected for his attempts to help his people and to communicate his vision to the dominant society and international forums. In his second book, *Eating Bitterness: A Vision beyond Prison Walls*, he describes the seven fires characterizing Ojibwa history to the present. The seventh fire is the time that the people "would retrace their steps to find the/sacred ways that had been left behind". It is also the time when:

> ... the light-skinned race would be given a choice,
> if they would choose the right road,
> then the seventh fire would light the eighth and final fire
> an eternal fire of peace, love, and brotherhood.[11]

The time for that choice is now. The teachings and power and medicines for the healing are available to all, but it requires action:

> If you want to find
> your healing
> in this land,
> you must learn
> that the medicine
> is in the teaching
> that says,
> "Thou shalt love thy neighbour
> as thyself."
>
> But you must understand
> that it will not help you
> or anyone else
> unless you use it.
>
> And the healing
> is in the doing,
> not in the talking.[12]

These solutions seem simple, but another respected Anishinabe elder taught that love is based on the principle that we should treat others not as we want others to do unto us but *as they want to be treated*. One of Solomon's foremost requirements is that:

> you will
> have to close your jails
> and accept us
> and treat us
> as Children of God.[13]

The Declaration of First Nations at the beginning of this chapter clearly states how Native peoples want to be treated. Support for the themes of that declaration is provided by the 1996 five-volume *Report of the Royal Commission on Aboriginal Peoples*, which includes a 105-page summary of recommendations. It begins with a thematic introductory statement in bold print: "The Commission recommends that a renewed relationship between Aboriginal and non-Aboriginal people in Canada be established on the basis of justice and fairness."[14] The statement is clear, but Aboriginal people agree that the process has not yet begun at any systemic level, and when we start talking about how to take steps to end colonization, tears come to their eyes. But tears are not enough; laughter is better and soon follows in these discussions because the heart cannot easily bear going into the pain. Laughter is part of the solution, as any visit to an Indian community will show, because "laughin' kinda frees up your insides an' you remember lot more things than if you get all sad an' weepy".[15]

In his novel *Keeper'n Me*, Ojibwa novelist and journalist Richard Wagamese creates the character of Keeper, an elder who is teaching a young man, Garnet Raven. Garnet returned to the reserve from Toronto and is learning both how to reintegrate into his community after having been torn from it by the Children's Aid Society and how to develop a positive relationship with the outside world that almost destroyed him. The novel is a vision of how healing within the community and a balanced relationship with Canadian society is possible in a modern world. Keeper says:

> I'm not talking about bringin' back the buffalo hunt or goin' back to the wigwam. I'm talkin' about passin' on the spirit of all things. If you got the spirit of the old way in you, well, you can handle most anythin' this new world got to throw around. The spirit of that life's our traditions. Things like respect, honesty, kindness and sharin'. Those are our traditions....
>
> Give respect, you give kindness, honesty, openness, gentleness, good thoughts, good actions. Simple, eh?
>
> That's what it's all about the Indyun way. Simplicity.[16]

At the heart of Keeper's teachings is the land, and Keeper explains that the tiny mole gets the most respect from his animal brothers and sisters because "he lives in constant touch with Mother Earth".[17] As Jeanette Armstrong, an Okanagan Salish poet and educator, explains, our language and teachings and survival and everything come from the land: "Language was given to us by the land we live in.... All my elders say that it is land that holds all knowledge of life and death and is a constant teacher.... Not to learn its language is to die."[18] If taken seriously, this idea alone makes colonization inconceivable.

A Salish author in British Columbia, Lee Maracle, explores the consequences of the symbolic and real river between a Salish community

and a white town in her novel *Ravensong*. The trickster character Raven
wants the isolation of the Native community to end because it threatens
their survival; she also wants an end to the white community's destruction of the land and their indifference to the suffering of the Salish community ever since contact. She wants the people in the white town to
start caring about what is happening across the river, and she wants the
Native people to go into white society to acquire solutions such as education and medicine. "Raven grew excited" because she sees the process
beginning with the Salish girl, Stacey, and the white teenager, Steve:
"Stacey had been the one to sow this seed in the heart of young Steve."[19]
That's where the new relationship that justice would require will probably have to begin – in the hearts of people who care.

Healing the individual in community

Many Aboriginal teachings about healing the spirit of individuals and
community are brought together in the readable and insightful book
Returning to the Teachings: Exploring Aboriginal Justice, by Rupert
Ross, a non-Aboriginal assistant crown attorney with the Canadian government, which funded his three-year study of Aboriginal approaches to
justice. The book emerged from the author's decade of experience on
over 20 remote Cree and Ojibway First Nations reserves, where he was
responsible for criminal prosecutions and learned that the mainstream
adversarial justice system usually failed Aboriginal communities.

Ross describes Aboriginal communities who use healing and so-
called sentencing circles to achieve higher degrees of success than the
government-provided justice system.[20] He also draws parallels with
peace-making in Navajo teachings as well as New Zealand's Family
Group Conference approach. This approach resulted in the closure of
half the young offender facilities in New Zealand and, in just five years
(from 1987 to 1992), a drop of 27 percent in the number of prosecuted
cases against young people aged 17-19.[21] The model of the sentenc-
ing/talking circle has also been successfully used to overcome disharmony between Native and non-Native individuals and groups.

The book throws light upon how First Nations communities take the
disharmony and broken relationships left by colonialism and, using their
traditional values, including a strong focus on relationship and process,
work constantly towards harmony and balance. Ross summarizes some
of the causes of the social breakdown that makes this necessary. Residential schools, he notes,

> were the closing punctuation mark in a loud, long declaration saying that noth-
> ing Aboriginal could possibly be of value to anyone. That message.... touched

every aspect of traditional social organization.... spiritual beliefs and practices, child-raising techniques, pharmacology, psychology, dispute resolution, decision making, clan organization or community governance.... [and] economic independence.

The law itself was implicated, having made it "illegal to possess medicine bundles, vote in Canadian elections, hold a potlatch to honour the assistance of others... hire a lawyer, or even *ask* a court to force governments to honour their treaty obligations".[22]

Growing out of their fundamental understanding that "all things are interrelated",[23] Ross perceived that Native healers seem to come down to one issue: connection and disconnection. "It's as if *some state of disconnection* (or unhealthy connection...) *is assumed to be the cause of the problem*, following which there will be lengthy investigation into how that state came to be and how all the processes that created it can be turned towards reconnection instead." In fact, Ross quotes Diane LeResche from the *Mediation Quarterly* to make the point that "peacemaking is more conciliation than it is mediation. It is relationship-centred, not agreement-centred.... Native American peace-making is inherently spiritual; it speaks to the connectedness of all things."[24]

Since we are all "substantially the products of our relationships", an offence in a Native community signals relational disharmonies that require healing for *both the individual and the community.* The traditional approach aims at providing healing for the mental, emotional, spiritual and physical health of all those affected. Hence the justice process must involve "all people within the web of relationships that surround every offender and every victim".[25] The purpose is healing, not punishment.

Ross observes that in Aboriginal communities, the process begins with the physical layout of the court. Instead of the accused and his lawyer sitting directly opposite the Crown and police, these people are placed in a *circle* with all interested parties, including translators, probation officers, alcohol workers, and family and friends of both the offender and the victim. All persons who want to make a contribution are involved because when an offence is committed in or against a Native community, "a real harm has been done to everyone". In the words of the 1993 Report of Grand Council Treaty no. 3, "Justice to our people means allegiance to the integrity of our spiritual principles and values." Thus the spiritual is at the heart of every action, and this value includes beginning all sessions with ceremony and prayer.[26]

Life for Aboriginal people is about process and the communication process with others supports individual dignity and self-esteem. In the circle everyone is given an equal, often formal, chance to participate, and everyone seems "committed to finding solutions that respect the contributions of all". This honouring of differing perspectives means that no single truth is expected to emerge, nor is a neutral, objective position possible. Value judgments appear to be relative, applying to the "*direction* in which things appear to be moving – towards or away from harmony".[27]

Ross learned the Ojibway teaching that healthy relationships and "a good life" depend on cultivating seven attributes: respect, caring, sharing, kindness, honesty, strength and humility. These virtues should be practised in relation to others, to oneself and to all creation. In dealing with people whose relationships have been built on power and abuse, one purpose of the sentencing circle is actually to give them the experience of relationships built on respect and the other attributes. This setting necessitates talking "from the heart". A position paper by one of the Aboriginal communities summarizes the values behind the sentencing circle as follows: "People who offend against another... are to be viewed and related to as people who are out of balance.... A return to balance can best be accomplished through a process of accountability that includes support from the community through teaching and healing."[28]

Whether healing/sentencing circles are trying to help someone overcome alcohol or drug abuse or are addressing issues of crime and violence, the pattern is the same: the spirit (spirituality) of the community infuses all actions taken, aiming towards harmony and balance for the individuals affected and the community as a whole. Healing takes place within community.

Healing the spirit within and between communities

On 27 October 1998 the moderator of the United Church of Canada offered an apology to the First Nations peoples of Canada for the church's involvement in operating the Indian Residential Schools. He added: "We must now seek ways of healing ourselves, as well as our relationships with First Nations peoples. This apology is not an end in itself. We are in the midst of a long and painful journey."[29] The journey of the churches and Aboriginal people referred to in this quotation began with contact. From the 1800s until the 1970s, the Government of Canada adopted a policy of "educating" Native children through Indian Residential Schools. The schools formed part of the government policy of assimilation – "to kill the Indian in the child" – that was explicitly stated until the 1960s.[30] Four churches were involved in operating the schools on a contractual basis with the federal government: Roman Catholic orders, Anglican, Presbyterian and United, the latter having inherited schools from Methodist and Presbyterian churches at union in 1925.

Until the middle of the 20th century, the churches explicitly supported the assimilationist goals. In the 1940s and 1950s thinking began
to change because of the harm to children in separating them from their
families and in light of the clear failure of assimilation ("Indian Residential School Background"). Since that time, all denominations have
taken steps to build bridges with First Nations people. In 1986 the
United Church delivered an apology at its General Council, acknowl-
edging, among other things, that "we confused western ways and culture
with... the gospel" ("Apology to First Nations").

After 1990 the churches and Canadian society began to hear the stories of former residential school students and their families.

An apology by the Anglican primate in 1993 responded on behalf of
the Anglican community, saying in part:

> I... know that I am in need of healing, and my own people are in need of heal-
> ing, and our church is in need of healing. Without that healing, we will con-
> tinue the same attitudes that have done such damage in the past.
>
> I know that healing takes a long time, both for people and for communities...
>
> I accept and I confess before God and you, our failures in the residential
> schools. We failed you. We failed ourselves. We failed God.
>
> I am sorry, more than I can say, that we were part of a system which took
> you and your children from home and family.
>
> I am sorry, more than I can say, that we tried to remake you in our image,
> taking from you your language and the signs of your identity.
>
> I am sorry, more than I can say, that in our schools so many were abused
> physically, sexually, culturally and emotionally.
>
> On behalf of the Anglican Church of Canada, I present our apology.[31]

The background document accompanying this apology states that
"the residential school as a system was a tool of oppression" and "a primary cause of the disintegration of native society", pointing in particular to the lasting damage brought by the break-up of families and the loss
of parenting skills. This apology, like that of the United Church, recognizes that much healing is necessary within the non-Aboriginal community before it can begin to heal relationships between the communities.
Apologies are only a small step along the road, and unlike the Native
community, where the need for healing is obvious in its rates of suicide,
alcoholism and other problems, the non-Native community does not easily recognize its need for healing. The federal government took a small
step in 1997, when it issued a Statement of Reconciliation, expressing its
"profound regret for past actions" and recognizing that "reconciliation is
an ongoing process".[32]

By mid-2000, Native people had filed nearly 9000 claims against the
government and the churches. Both United and Anglican churches said

that the possible resulting financial obligations could spell bankruptcy for them. The United Church observed, however, that the more important question was a spiritual one ("Residential School Litigation"), and the moderator stated that "the whole church and the whole of Canadian society must take hold of this shameful part of our history in order to be able to build a more hopeful future for our relationship with Canada's First Nations" ("A Pastoral Letter from the Moderator"). The same document points out that "the path of healing and reconciliation is a long one. It will take many generations to mend the relationships."

The suggestions made at the beginning of this chapter by Aboriginal people about enhancing the spirit of community with a view to building bridges between communities could serve the church well. The first two suggestions are that the people in each community get together to discuss what to do and that they begin with spirituality.

Their final suggestion is careful *listening* followed by *action*, not just words. Listening, a dominant value in First Nations culture, is not typical of Eurocentric cultures.[33] When non-Aboriginal Canadians listen "from the heart" to First Nations people, the actions that are needed will become obvious.

The spirit of community

How we take the first step to learn from Aboriginal people is important. For them, it is learning to do things "in a good way". An Anishinabe elder was asked, "What do you say when white people come with questions and don't even offer tobacco?" He said, "It doesn't happen as often as it used to. Most people now find out first how to approach elders with respect, but I usually just say, in a gentle voice, 'I don't know'."

The First People of Turtle Island (North America) are working hard to heal their communities and have learned a great deal about Canadian people and their ways. They are patiently waiting for an opening of hearts from the visitors who came offering the Bible and soon took their land. One of the meanings of the word "Anishinabe" is someone who is "a good person", which, among other things, includes welcoming any guests with respect according to the traditional teachings. Thus sweat lodges are normally open and the medicines available to those who ask in a good way. First Nations communities welcome visitors to their healing lodge circles to talk and listen around the sacred fire. This gathering usually involves a lot of preparation and effort. The lodge has to be built, medicines and wood are needed for the fire, someone must prepare an opening ceremony and so on to make sure that it will all be done in a good way. The elders are available day and night to do what needs to get done when someone asks.

There are noteworthy similarities between First Nations approaches and the concept of *ubuntu* as espoused by Archbishop Desmond Tutu of South Africa. Ubuntu expresses the idea that "we can be human only in community" and that "each individual's humanity is ideally expressed in relation with others". Theologian Michael Battle explains that "*ubuntu* refers to the person who is welcoming, who is hospitable, who is warm and generous, who is affirming of others".[34] For both First Nations people and African philosophy, body and spirit are experienced as two parts of a single whole. Both thus understand that any kind of harm to the person harms the spirit. That damaged spirit damages the community spirit; hence, for each of us, wholeness depends on the degree to which others realize their potential. There seems to be a profound understanding in both *ubuntu* theology and among First Nations people that for a community to become whole, the individuals within it must experience healing.

First Nations peoples are doing what they can to heal and strengthen their spirit as individuals and as communities. The possibility for a new beginning still exists because they and their way of life survive. It is time that we can laugh together with a happy heart. George Blondin, a Dene statesman and author, says in his book *Yamoria the Lawmaker: Stories of the Dene*, "Had my ancestors been given a chance to show the newcomers what they knew, life would probably be a lot different today."[35] It challenges the imagination to consider what the world would be like today if the first and subsequent invaders from Europe had come as visitors with respect. Our experience suggests that they would have received so much more than they stole, including, most of all, gifts of the spirit that cannot be stolen and can hardly be imagined.

We still have the choice of making a new beginning.[36] And listening will be a major part of that process. We heard a young man come to an Oneida woman and ask, "I just found out my grandfather was a chief. What can I do because I don't know anything about what it means to be an Indian?" She answered, "Your heart already knows what your first step has to be. Take that step and then wait until it shows you the next one. Of course we have longhouses where you can go and get help and teachings if you need them." The same teaching might apply for anyone who really wants to begin to work towards a new and healthy relationship between the original peoples of the land and the Canadian settlers.[37]

NOTES

[1] The term "First Nations" is used interchangeably with "Aboriginal", "Indian" and "Native persons". All of these are terms used by First Nations themselves. *Anishinabe* is an indigenous word used to refer to Algonquian people, including the Ojibwa, Potawatomi, Odawa and other First Nations people.

[2] Adopted by the Joint Council of Chiefs and Elders, Dec. 1980, taken from an unpublished flyer. The text is also available with minor changes as "A Declaration of First Nations" on the Assembly of First Nations web site. The declaration also forms the Preamble to the Charter of the Assembly of First Nations. See "About the AFN" at http://www.afn.ca/eng_main.htm.

[3] Kateri Akiwenzie-Damm, "We Belong to This Land: A View of 'Cultural Difference'", in *Literary Pluralities,* ed. Christl Verduyn, Peterborough, Broadview Press/*Journal of Canadian Studies,* 1998, pp.84-85.

[4] Penny Petrone, ed., *First People, First Voices,* Toronto, Univ. of Toronto Press, 1987, p.106.

[5] Quoted from Ernest Thomas Seton's introduction to *The Shagganappi,* in David Daniel Moses and Terry Goldie, *An Anthology of Canadian Native Literature in English,* 2nd ed., Toronto, Oxford UP, 1998, p.506.

[6] *Ibid.,* p.29.

[7] Conversation with the authors, Jan. 2000.

[8] A.C. Hamilton and C.M. Sinclair, *Report of the Aboriginal Justice Inquiry of Manitoba,* vol. 1, *The Justice System and Aboriginal People,* Province of Manitoba, 1991, pp.162,169.

[9] Armand Garnet Ruffo, "Why Native Literature?", in *Native North America: Critical and Cultural Perspectives,* ed. Reneé Hulan, Toronto, ECW Press, 1999, p.110.

[10] C. Murray Sinclair, "Suicide in First Nations People", in *Suicide in Canada,* ed. A.A. Leenaars et al., Toronto, Univ. of Toronto Press, 1998, p.177.

[11] Arthur Solomon, *Eating Bitterness: A Vision beyond the Prison Walls. Poems and Essays,* eds Cathleen Kneen and Michael Poslums, Toronto, NC Press, 1994, p.15.

[12] *Ibid.,* p.64.

[13] *Ibid.,* p.65.

[14] Government of Canada, *Report of the Royal Commission on Aboriginal Peoples,* 5 vols, Canada Communication Group, 1996, 5:141.

[15] Richard Wagamese, *Keeper'n Me,* Toronto, Doubleday Canada, 1995, p.150.

[16] *Ibid.,* pp.37,116.

[17] *Ibid.,* p.152.

[18] Jeanette Armstrong, "Land Speaking", in *Speaking for the Generations: Native Writers on Writing,* ed. Simon J. Ortitz, Tucson, Univ. of Arizona Press, 1998, pp.175-76.

[19] Lee Maracle, *Ravensong: A Novel,* Vancouver, Press Gang Publishers, 1993, p.191.

[20] We are grateful to First Nations author Rolland Nadjiwon for a very thoughtful response to the sentencing-circles process described here. He points out that "the problems we experience, as a people, are imported.... Most offences that 'natives' commit are not against each other (although physical abuse is on the increase), they are offences against laws that are imposed upon us." Nadjiwon notes that Native people are not in control of many of the choices surrounding sentencing circles. for example, funding depends on the government and the Crown attorney decides which crimes or individuals will come before the sentencing circle. Nadjiwon explains that "ideas that are not ours cannot begin to fit into our ways. There needs to be a new recognition of our own laws which are based on sharing, kindness, love, caring, and so on. I don't know if that can happen; it has never been tried. Upon contact we were, and have since been, the recipients of foreign imperialism. It has nothing in common with how most of our peoples saw our world, universe, cosmology" (email communication, 17 March 2000).

[21] Rupert Ross, *Returning the Teachings: Exploring Aboriginal Justice,* Toronto, Penguin Books, 1996, p.23.

[22] *Ibid.,* pp.46-48,123.

[23] *The Sacred Tree,* quoted in *ibid.,* p.134.

[24] *Ibid.,* pp.135,68.

[25] *Ibid.,* pp.270-71.

[26] *Ibid.,* pp.7-8,18,257,35.

[27] *Ibid.,* pp.83,87-88,123.

[28] *Ibid.,* pp.149-50,171-72.

[29] "United Church Apologizes for Its Complicity in the Indian Residential School System", United Church of Canada web site (http://www.uccan.org/). The other documents cited below in the text are also available at this web site.

[30] Government of Canada, *Report,* 5:365.

[31] "Apology and Acceptance: A Message from the Primate, Archbishop Michael Peers, to the National Native Convocation, Minaki, Ont., 1993", Anglican Church of Canada web site (http://www.anglican.ca).

32 We understand the objection of some first Nations people to the term "reconciliation" because its meaning can include the assumption that there was a time when the relationship was good. Although there have been and are good relationships between Native and non-Native individuals that may have extended to the community, these relationships are always systemically in the context of colonialism.

33 Ella Shohat and Robert Stam's book *Unthinking Eurocentrism: Multiculturalism and the Media*, London, Routledge, 1994, provides an excellent analysis of the characteristics of Eurocentrism.

34 Michael Battle, *Reconciliation: The Ubuntu Theology of Desmond Tutu*, Cleveland, Pilgrim Press, 1997, pp.5,39,35.

35 George Blondin, *Yamoria the Lawmaker: Stories of the Dene*, Edmonton, NeWest Press, 1997, p.vi.

36 A discussion of one of the numerous plans for reconciliation appears at http://www.wmat.nsn.us/reconcil.htm, entitled "Reconciliation, Community Healing, and Ndee La' Ade' – the Great Fort Apache Heritage Reunion".

37 We the authors, Canadians of European descent, are acutely aware that we can perceive the teachings we have received from Aboriginal people only through the filters of our own culture. We are very grateful to Anishinabe friends and teachers Rolland Nadjiwon and Elizabeth Chamberlain for valuable comments on this chapter. We thank the Anishinabek communities in Ontario and many others throughout Turtle Island for welcoming us as visitors, especially Garden River First Nation Indian Reserve, and the many people who have taught us about their ways, including elders and others who do not wish to be called elders or do not think of themselves that way. We also thank the United Church of Canada for opening a path to First Nations people at the 1986 General Council, when they decided to present the apology; we also thank Native organizations such as the Can-Am Indian Friendship Centre in Windsor and the students and staff at Turtle Island Aboriginal Education Centre at the University of Windsor. We thank the people of the land whom we visited in Aotearoa (New Zealand), Australia and the Caribbean Islands, including the Carib Reserve in Dominica, as well as all the people who joined in the struggle to end apartheid in South Africa, proving that the seemingly impossible is possible.

Communicating Disability as a Human Rights Issue

JAHDA ABOU KHALIL AND NAWAF KABBARA

Is disability a human rights issue? Are the violations of the rights of people with disabilities a human rights concern? Many readers may be surprised that these questions are ever posed. We have every reason to argue, however, that the cause of disability is not yet a serious matter of concern for human rights activists, agencies and organizations. In 1975 the UN indeed passed an international charter on the rights of disabled people. And the UN General Assembly declared the year 1981 to be the International Year of Disability and agreed to declare an International Decade of Disability in the years 1983-92, which would be followed by a world programme of action concerning disability.

There is a problem, however. At a meeting in Stockholm of world-wide experts on disability and organizations of people with disabilities, held in November 2000, representatives of the UN Commission on Human Rights and of different UN agencies stated clearly that disability is not yet on their agenda as a human rights issue. They also revealed that even though different UN declarations and discourses have started to acknowledge disability as a human rights concern, UN agencies in fact have not yet started to tackle the issue and do not know how to deal with it. The meeting also revealed that the UN special rapporteur on disability works independently from other agencies. In particular, the rapporteur operates without any form of coordination with different UN human rights commissions and agencies.

Furthermore, our experience as activists in the field of disability in the Arab world and in the international arena reveals clearly that disability is not yet on the agenda of human rights organizations, including feminist movements, minority rights groups and other related agencies. Every time these organizations conduct a certain activity or produce a policy document or statement, organizations of people with disabilities have to lobby hard to ensure that their cause is being mentioned or possibly included in the statements and programmes of these organizations. Some examples may clarify the assertion.

At the 1995 Beijing Conference on Women, the issue of women with disability was not on the agenda of different feminist organizations.

Activists for women with disability had to lobby hard and fight to ensure that their cause was included in the programme of the conference – without too much success in either the process or the results. Furthermore, a UNESCO conference on adult education that took place in 1997 in Hamburg, Germany, agreed under pressure from the representatives of different organizations of people with disabilities to convene a conference in 1999 to discuss the special educational needs of adult persons with disabilities. The conference, however, never took place.

Similar negligence can be observed in programmes related to child rights projects and care. The problems of children with disability are not seriously tackled within the programmes and plans of UNICEF and the various non-governmental organizations (NGOs) dealing with child issues. Even though we may find some support for programmes that cater for the problems of children with disability, the budgets allocated to such programmes are much less than those reserved for other programmes and projects. How can we explain such a phenomenon?

Ghettoizing disability

It seems that in relation to the question of disability, the ghetto concept is still dominant in the strategy of different agencies and organizations, including those dealing with human rights issues. This ghetto approach to disability seems to be based on the idea that disability issues must be discussed and negotiated separately from other issues. Accordingly, most agencies working in the human rights field do not consider themselves directly concerned with, or responsible for, the human rights violations of people with disabilities. Organizations active in the public domain include those monitoring human rights, feminist issues and children's rights, yet disability is still outside their concerns. The main factors that seem to be directing these organizations' approaches to disability can be summarized as follows:

- Disability is not a question of oppression but of medical care and rehabilitation. Accordingly, people with disabilities do not constitute a social identity that can be politically addressed and dealt with but are an issue for the attention of the welfare state and its departments.
- Based on the above, it is up to medical, rehabilitation and social workers and administrators to represent the interests of people with disabilities and to define and determine the parameters of the issue. What is to be done with the population of a country who have disabilities is simply to provide the needed medical and social support for their welfare, including institutional support and community-based rehabilitation.

- People with disabilities may be represented through NGOs. Disability politics and discourse, however, are determined out of a partnership among these organizations and other active non-disabled bodies in the field.

The background of this ghetto mentality reflects the history of disability as an issue and a cause. In fact, the history of the views on disability goes back professionally to the development of the medical sciences and psychology. Prior to this period, ignorance and superstition were the dominant elements of the discourse on disability in any society. People with disabilities were regarded as having a sign of an evil spirit or of the work of the devil, or of having received a punishment. The treatment of disability was very much in the hands of religious people and institutions. At best, people with disabilities were thrown into what was known in the 16th and 17th centuries as hospitals or asylums. These institutions were where society hid away all people considered abnormal.

The development of medical sciences and psychology has drastically shifted the discourse concerning disability. People with disabilities were no longer considered to have evil spirits but were seen as medical cases that needed special attention and treatment. Institutions were created for this purpose, and over time specialized institutions in each category of disability were established. These institutions became places where families released the burden of disability from their own shoulders and threw it back onto those of the institutions. A person with a disability became confined most of his or her life within these institutions. It was a time when the welfare state started to develop, with an increasing role for the state as the body in charge of the health of all its citizens. It was believed that medically, people with disabilities had to be under state supervision and patronage in sponsored and financed institutions. Religious institutions in charge of welfare and care developed similar model institutions. This framework was dominant in the West until the end of the 1960s and is still very much alive in many Third World countries, including the Arab world.

By the early 1970s a change in thinking started to take place with regard to the governmental and societal approach to disability. The new discourse viewed disability as a societal phenomenon, not as a medical issue. According to the logic of this new approach, there is no society in history and in real life that disabled people do not form part of. The issue is therefore not one of cure but one of integration and acceptance. The main reason why disability continues to be a problem is society's refusal to acknowledge people with disabilities as full and equal members of its fabric. Thus, if society suffers from discriminatory cultures based on sexism, racism and so forth, we can now add a new "ism" called "disabilitism", namely, the tendency to discriminate against people with disabilities in all aspects of their life, including the law, jobs, education, access to transport and so on.

New public discourses

Many factors led to change. To begin with, one must look at the global mind-set that was governing society, culture and political development in Western countries during the 1960s. That was the period when civil rights discourse entered the intellectual and political life of Western societies. The American black non-violence movement, feminism, the anti-establishment revolution and liberal socialism were examples of the new trend in American and Western societies. Disability, however, was still outside the framework of most of these changes and new intellectual trends. The Vietnam War was a turning point helping to make disabilities an issue of human and civil rights. The war produced a huge number of young disabled persons who refused to be treated as marginalized people or to be institutionalized all their life. In addition, the war created a strong feeling of guilt and responsibility in American society towards war veterans and soldiers with disabilities.

By the early 1970s a combination of increasing protest by Americans with disabilities and governmental concern led to the development of a new view of disability. This new approach placed the problem and misery of people with disabilities within society itself and not on the medical and mental status of the persons themselves. What society needed was not more institutions and medical control over the life of such people but the introduction of major changes in social structures to ensure their real integration. This discursive shift was developed and promoted through the work of prominent Americans with disabilities. These pioneers formed what became known in the USA as Independent Living Centers.

The first centre was formed in Berkeley, California. Run by people with disabilities themselves, it promoted a new approach to their care. Services and special needs of persons with disabilities were henceforth to be addressed through local offices providing these people with support to make them independent. Advocacy and peer counselling became the basis of the work of all the independent living centres. Empowerment of people with disability became one of their main targets. One essential form of empowerment was the development of an alternative discourse to that of care and institutionalization. The new approach shifted the responsibility of disability affairs from doctors and institutions to the society at large.

The new approach spoke of integration. Marginalization of people with disabilities, according to this new trend of thought, was not the result of their physical and mental conditions but the product of the insensitivity of society to the needs of these people, in terms of both social attitudes and failure to provide physical accessibility. The question of disability became one of human rights and tolerance.

Social economics enters the picture

If the Vietnam War was a major catalyst behind the change, another specific reason has contributed to changing attitudes. Even though one may assume that the Left and liberal parties are more open and supportive of disability rights than conservatives and right-wing parties, the latter were open and positive to this new approach out of both patriotism (feelings towards war veterans and heroes) and economics. It has been proved that caring for people with disabilities in institutions is very expensive. The rise of right-wing ideology in most of the West during the 1980s has put under scrutiny the whole concept of the welfare state and the degree of needed state intervention in social affairs. Spending cuts for social issues implied the need to rethink all of the social system. Disability was one of the issues that needed to be reviewed, given its high cost to society. Such a review coincided with the new conclusion that societal integration and rehabilitation are more rewarding and productive. Instead of paying for the confinement of people with disabilities for life in institutions, let us make society more accessible to them and train them for productive jobs.

Fortunately and unfortunately, however, the response of medical and rehabilitation institutions to this new trend was to develop the concept of community-based rehabilitation (CBR). This approach was a reasonable solution proposed by professionals without disabilities working in the disability field to the new challenges produced by the new discourse. CBR acknowledged the merit and superiority of integration. At the same time, it gave professionals the dominant role as rehabilitators and directors of disability issues. It is not surprising that the CBR concept was first developed in the United Nations, which worked to promote it worldwide, showing clearly that the UN was very much under the influence of the professionals and not of disabled people themselves, who would surely opt for an approach based more on an independent living model. CBR, however, was no doubt a revolutionary approach in comparison with the medical institutional model of the first half of the century.

Like the independent living approach, CBR programmes work at using available resources in the community to provide accessibility and integration for the person with a disability. However, whereas people with disabilities have the upper hand in the independent living structure, social workers, psychologists, physiotherapists and other related professionals work with such a person in his or her community to provide needed services. The rehabilitation strategy focuses on getting the person ready to take control of his or her life.

The main strength of the independent living approach is that it is run by people with disabilities and works to introduce major changes in favour of people with disabilities in the legal and public policies of the country. It is thus a lobbying activity aimed at enabling people with disabilities to become active political players and participants in the social life of the country. The CBR approach, however, focuses on rehabilitation and self-reliance, but without any real attempt to empower the people themselves. Nevertheless, CBR has still proved to be very useful in developing countries where one can use the tools and resources available to make rehabilitation possible. There is no longer any need for sophisticated centres and equipment to rehabilitate people with disabilities within institutions, but we can use very simple tools from the local community to reach the same objective.

Empowerment and identity

Both the independent living centres and the CBR concept and programmes are based on the formation of a small bureau or office run by social workers in the community or local environment where people with disabilities want to work. The task of this group is to locate disabled people, determine their needs and survey the area to find out what resources are available (both human and economic) that can be used to support them. The goal is to match the needs of people with disabilities with possible opportunities and rehabilitation facilities within the community itself. Creating local volunteers, changing people's attitudes through a process of continual negotiation, integrating people with disabilities into mainstream education (dependent on the type of disability) and providing job training and job opportunities within the community are all part of the plan. Accordingly, all of these centres are a form of partnership among three groups: social workers, local volunteers and people with disabilities. The difference is that in the independent living model, disabled people themselves determine the agenda and programmes, whereas in the CBR model, persons without disabilities take charge.

Without doubt, the role of the state and local government is vital to the success of these programmes. It is up to government to issue regulations and laws to make the concept of integration possible at different levels within the nation. It is also the role of both state and local government to enforce such regulations and to provide funds and resources to make integration successful. In this domain, the difference between the two models becomes essential. Only through empowering people with disabilities and building disability as a social identity can the cause of disability be addressed as a political and human rights issue. Only people with disabilities themselves are ready to fight and make sacrifices for their own cause. A CBR worker or activist is interested in providing much-needed social and welfare support, whereas a person with disability is interested in alleviating all forms of discrimination against him or her as a human being and citizen that undermine his or her right to full participation in the social and political life of a country.

The degree of development in the field of disability differs from one country to another, and from one society to another. As far as the Third World is concerned, including the Arab world, it seems to us that the three above-mentioned approaches towards disability are still alive in these societies and countries. Some of the rural and poor areas still look at disability as the work of the devil or an evil spirit. Others still believe in the medical paradigm of disability and the need for institutionalization to provide continual care. This attitude is still very dominant in many Arab and Third World countries.

The concept of CBR programmes and of integration, however, is also spreading rapidly in this region of the world. So far, though, most programmes are the product of private initiatives or the result of intervention by the UN and by international NGOs. Parallel to the emergence of different CBR programmes and projects, organizations of people with disabilities are also springing up in many Third World countries, including the Arab world. Unfortunately, this development is not often attributable to local factors and the struggle of such people themselves. One reason behind the development of these organizations is outside intervention and support. Western organizations of persons with disabilities are successful in supporting the development of such organizations in the Third World and have succeeded in lobbying international donors to provide funds for this purpose.

A combination of both international change and local pressure has led many Third World countries, including those in the Arab world, to pass laws and regulations that support the idea of the protection and integration of people with disabilities. Unfortunately, governments are not vigorous enough in applying such laws and in providing enough resources for the implementation of programmes to eliminate barriers to the integration of these people into their societies. The combined efforts of the UN, regional bodies such as the Arab League, and different NGO representatives of people with disabilities themselves can play a very positive role in promoting the idea of integration and CBR within Third World countries.

Media as a tool for change

Finally, a great deal of effort is needed to place disability as a human rights issue high on the agenda of concerned organizations and agencies. No doubt, awareness of the question has risen tremendously in the last ten years. This positive change of attitude, however, should coincide with a similar change in programmes, plans and laws to make this new social discourse of integration and human rights a reality. One of the major tools for change is a strategy for proactive use of the media. In the past, the media were used to reinforce the traditional approach towards disability. Furthermore, many prominent journalists and TV reporters have portrayed disability negatively when they were attacking something or criticizing certain programmes or governments. They might refer to a government or parliament as "handicapped". One recent example of these media abuses of disability issues was an article published in Ireland by a prominent journalist attacking the Paralympics and ridiculing the sport efforts and activities of people with disabilities.

Media attitudes can be changed if people with disabilities prove themselves a serious force in society. In 1987 a march of Lebanese people with disabilities against the war and violence in Lebanon was a very innovative and courageous move. This action encouraged all national and international media to focus on the role of such people in Lebanon as agents of peace and pioneers against war and violence in the country. Furthermore, organizations of people with disabilities must find a professional way of dealing with the media and of monitoring media abuse against themselves. One way is to form clearing houses to deal with the media, as was recommended at the recent meeting in Stockholm. Such centres publish different forms of magazines and other publications. They also monitor what is written or broadcast by different media outlets and react to it.

People with disabilities must work to change the language and approaches to disability. Positive approaches towards them by the media are not going to be achieved without organizations of people with disabilities working seriously and consistently with the media to reach this goal. In the end, it is up to people with disabilities themselves to ensure that their cause is registered as a human rights issue. Clearly things are much better now. But people with disabilities may lose what they have already achieved if they do not continue to invest their strengths effectively and intelligently towards the goal of humanizing their cause.

The Politics of Reconciliation:
A Story from India

V. GEETHA

Truth, justice, forgiveness and reconciliation: ethical norms from a different and earlier era have become part of political discourse in many parts of the world today. The pope pleads for forgiveness for the intended and unintended misdemeanours of the church; the Truth and Reconciliation Commission in South Africa desperately affirms the need to remember crimes committed under apartheid, if only to forgive and forget.

If some seek absolution for their crimes, others demand confessions and remorse from those who are obdurately silent about their actions in the past – the Koreans want the Japanese to apologise for war crimes, many people around the world want America to admit that Vietnam was a disaster and a wrong.

These gestures and sentiments have emerged at a historical moment that is eager to collapse the past into an imagined future of world plenty and harmony. Spurred by fantasies of global togetherness and wealth, exhorted by the possibilities of unlimited and seamless communication and an integrated world market, political leaders and intellectuals across countries appear insistent that we put aside memories of exploitation and underdevelopment, violence and extortion, racism and death. The future, we are told, must eschew ideology and adopt a pragmatic and sensible approach towards survival and coexistence.

To people tired of war and want, exhausted by political struggles that demand long, dreary periods of suffering, endurance, violence and penury, these offers of reconciliation are attractive. Acrimony and hatred tire the aching, fighting heart, stun it into numbness.

A future of remorse?

Is forgiveness easy? Can one actually live, in good faith, with one's (former?) tormentors? Can reconciliation in the present moment guarantee a future that will not repeat the miseries of the past? These questions are troubling and difficult to address, partly because the discursive context that has given rise to them is riddled with internal contradictions.

To express remorse and ask for forgiveness are deeply penitential acts, whose meaning assumes significance only when validated by signs and rituals of penance and mortification. Historically, such acts have come about as the result of individual moral choices, with the individual in question opting for both a symbolic and an actual renunciation of material comfort and personal hatred, a public expression of guilt and sorrow and the adoption of a private humility. Today's gestures of public remorse seek to acquire for themselves the poignancy that is inherent to penitential acts without actually giving it material form and coherence.

In any case, expressions of individual remorse, or even guilt, cannot explore options for redress that would compensate for the past, in a real, material and collective sense. They cannot because penitence and contrition are experiences informed by a phenomenological, rather than political, sensibility. Critical observers of South Africa's Truth and Reconciliation Commission (TRC) have pointed out that the whole notion of guilt that was invoked during the commission's hearings lacked credibility. This was because of the very nature of the emotion: "Guilt can... be ascribed only individually and not collectively. It is doubtful whether a 'traumatized' nation can be cured by having a repressed memory restored. Medical metaphors are misleading when applied to collectivities."[1]

Besides, the emotive rhetoric of individual guilt and sorrow in the South African situation and other instances often impales itself on a recounting of horror, without critically examining the conditions that created that horror. In his essay on the Truth and Reconciliation Commission, Alexander draws attention to one of the most eloquent and subtle criticisms of the commission:

> Part epistemological and methodological, part moral, the effect of these discursive strategies [adopted by the commission] is to produce a primarily descriptive rendition of the past, uneven in its discernment of detail and indifferent to the complexities of social causation. The TRC's "truth" about the past is neither "complex" nor particularly "extensive" (despite its length). With little explanatory and analytical power, the report reads less as a history, more as a moral narrative about the fact of moral wrongdoing across the political spectrum, spawned by the overriding evil of the apartheid system.

More generally, can the demand and desire for reconciliation restore to the tormented and abused a sense of personal, public, social and economic worth? Alexander continues:

> [How] can South Africans reconcile "the black demand for majority rule [with] white concerns stemming from this demand"? How can the redistribution of resources and opportunities occur without the destruction of the economy? How can South Africa protect the rights of its white citizens without entrenching the privileges of old? How can the cultural rights of groups be rec-

onciled with a broader national project? How is equity possible in the face of
continuing disparities in housing, education, income, media control, in the
broad cultural and linguistic dominance of a demographic minority? How is
justice possible when perpetrators of terrible crimes and human rights abuses
can walk away through amnesty?

There is a further problem. Those who are the objects of remorse and
reconciliation have neither the political energy and resources nor the
authority to enforce penitence. They can ignore these grand gestures
seeking absolution or answer them with their own brand of public, moral
politics – for instance, holding public hearings that would announce to
the world the crimes committed against them, whether in the name of
Christianity and progress, or slavery and racism; or lobbying and nego-
tiating in international forums for justice and compensation. Several
social action groups in parts of Africa and South Asia have done the latter – daring to name the perpetrators of misdeeds, demanding accountability and sentencing, compensation and remorse.

In many instances, though, moral anger, rather than political reason-
ing, sustains these criticisms and the demands that accompany them,
grounded though they are in good faith and hard work. Even when public tribunals are organized locally, they do not provoke serious public
debate on the subject in question. For instance, in India, beginning from
the mid-1990s, several public hearings have been held on violence
against women. These sessions bring together the victims of violence
and their supporters, sometimes even officers of the state. The victims
narrate their tales of woe and ask for justice and compensation. A jury,
comprising lawyers, human rights activists and concerned citizens, asks
for better enforcement of existing laws and sometimes demands new
laws. The jury also draws attention to the social and cultural determi-
nants of violence and suggests that judicial action alone will not alter
existing conditions of inequality and oppression. It calls for transformation in civil society and demands the political empowerment of women.
State officials, if present, solemnly pledge their word that they will
enforce the law without prejudice and will render all possible help to
those women who approach them.

Essentially, though, the hearings remain a bounded affair. They are
not convened to persuade the public of the rightness of a cause – very
rarely do the man and woman on the street walk into these hearings.
Media reports merely repeat what they have seen and heard but seldom
rework the arguments for a public debate. Besides, a hearing is a unique
event; its efforts cannot be endlessly repeated or sustained. These hearings are limited in another sense as well. The tribunal that hears tales of

wrongdoing and injustice is not a court of law. It cannot summon witnesses, haul up wrongdoers. Even when such a tribunal passes strictures against the perpetrators of wrong, it does not possess the authority to act on its findings. It can direct the law to a particular purpose, but it cannot mandate and enforce judicial action.

What function do the hearings serve? They enable women to speak out, offer them a public space to cry and mourn, rendering their sorrow visible and transparent. The presence of a jury instils confidence in the women; more important, the jury publicly affirms their rights to freedom and equality. Clearly, the hearings enable a catharsis, an expulsion of anger, fear, anxiety and grief. In this sense, a public tribunal is not really a judicial or civic space. It is public theatre at its rawest, enabling a play of moral rather than political and social reason.

What happens to just causes in international forums? Exhortations to justice that are voiced in global forums do not really affect life in the actual social sites where acts of violence and injustice routinely take place. Some Indian social action groups that work with and represent Dalits (the so-called untouchables) have lately taken their case to international forums.[2] Their plight has attracted the attention of groups such as Human Rights Watch. This strategic move has granted visibility to an issue that the Indian state would like to treat as a minor aberration in an otherwise functioning democracy. Appealing thus to an abstract, global conscience, however, has also successfully displaced the issue in question from its constituent context – an embattled everyday – and on to one that is given to resolving matters through advocacy and lobbying, rather than a sustained struggle. The uncertain rewards of political struggle are thus exchanged – even if momentarily – for the more expressive power of political visibility.

Trial by spectacle

This reading of the current discourse and practice of reconciliation politics is not a cynical one; rather, it is inspired by a sense of dismay at the subsuming of political action within the matrix of political performance. Though it is only a moment, an aspect of a sustained struggle, the performance, whether as strategy or tactic, answers to a script that is not entirely governed by the ultimate objectives of the struggle. For this script is dictated as much by the logic of the stage, by the aesthetics of spectacle, as it is by the cause it expounds. Commenting on the "dramaturgy" of the Truth Commission, Neville Alexander points out that the whole exercise is problematic, though fascinating. Pointing to the phenomenon of white middle-class men being questioned, he observes:

Whether it was intended or not, this imagery was and is reminiscent of a victorious revolutionary movement accusing the perpetrators and traitors of the previous regime and there is little doubt that dragon's teeth were and are being sown here. The sense of humiliation induced by this procedure will at some point in the future find expression in cyclical violence or some other conflictual reaction.

In the case of Indian Dalits, the problem is neither as dramatic nor as acute, since the tribunals that heard them were located elsewhere, and the Indian upper castes have not been asked to be bodily present to answer for their sins. The problem of humiliation remains, however, but with very different implications. Though the upper castes in India have not been asked seriously to examine themselves and their consciences, they have been named as criminals. They are bound to read these indictments of their actions as a slur on their honour and a challenge to their pride. In many parts of India, upper caste violence against Dalits over the last decade has been the result of anger, provoked by Dalit assertion, an anger that reflects a contested authority, as much as it does an offended sensibility. Besides being destructive and hateful, this violence successfully disables all further reflections on the subject. It induces a series of denials and justifications, and once the guns are silent and the massacres over, violence comes to rest in the moral sophistry that the unrepentant upper castes continually advance to deny their own complicity.

Can one imagine and enact a politics of performance that enables deep self-reflection and social transformation? Can one elicit an acceptance of guilt and complicity on the part of the oppressors that translates into contrition and compensation in a real, material sense? As Neville Alexander asks: "How to move towards understanding without ever forgetting, but to remember without constantly rekindling the divisive passions of the past? Such an approach is the only one which would allow us to look down into the darkness of the well of the atrocities of the past and to speculate on their causes at the same time as we haul up the waters of hope for a future with dignity and equality."

Do we have precedents in the Indian context that may stimulate us to push and expand the limits to a politics of reconciliation? I wish to address these questions in the context of two kinds of responses to the moral and social evil that is untouchability.

Mahatma Gandhi became a prominent figure in the Indian freedom movement in the second decade of the 20th century. He brought to politics a sense of moral seriousness by insisting that the struggle against British rule must simultaneously address inequities within Indian society. One of the problems that he consistently addressed during this period and after had to do with untouchability. He argued that every

Hindu must search deep within his or her conscience and wholeheartedly realize that untouchability was morally wrong. Only such a realization, backed by self-awareness, he held, would lead to true remorse, which, in turn, had to be expressed by acts of atonement and penance: "Should not we the Hindus wash our blood-stained hands before we ask the English to wash theirs?"[3]

Since untouchability was sustained by an abject lowness imposed on the castes that laboured as scavengers and toilet cleaners, upper-caste Hindus must begin performing these tasks themselves, if only to realize that there was nothing demeaning about them. In other words, Gandhi held that upper-caste Hindus must undergo an act of ritual and ethical purification by acquainting themselves with dirt, by in fact taking to it, as a penitential act. To atone for their sins towards the untouchables, they had to become one of them. Speaking at a conference of untouchables, Gandhi remarked:

> I do not want to be reborn. But if I have to be reborn, I should be born an untouchable, so that I may share their sorrows, sufferings and the affronts levelled at them in order that I may endeavour to free myself and them from that miserable condition.... I love scavenging. In my ashram an eighteen year old Brahmin lad is doing the scavenger's work in order to teach the Ashram scavenger cleanliness. The lad is not reformer. He was born and bred in orthodoxy.... But he felt that his accomplishments were incomplete until he became also a perfect sweeper, and that, if he wanted the Ashram sweeper to do his work, he must do it himself and set an example. You should realize that you are cleaning Hindu society. (202)

Gandhi aligned atonement with truthful knowing. He argued that acts of penitence required an unflinching commitment to a struggle for the truth, a truth that is not given to one but that each individual must seek and discover in the loneliness of his or her inner world. This struggle was the war for truth, or *satyagraha*, which an individual waged with himself or herself and the world.

Gandhi's campaigns against untouchability were of a part with the rest of his political sensibility. He relied on highly experiential notions of personal reflection and conscience-heeding, rectitude and penance to articulate his personal as well as public ethics. Personal ethical choices were granted salience by being endowed with a political and social resonance, while public choices with regard to social and political issues were enlivened and rendered meaningful by an expressive moral vigour. Effective political action ultimately depended on individual moral effort, on an ethics of self-cultivation. Several hundred individual wills, animated by a feeling for *satyagraha,* made up the political collective.

Gandhi's passionate espousal of the cause of untouchables was as much due to his strong sense of himself as a Hindu as it was to his revulsion against the practice of untouchability. Representing himself as a Hindu was important for Gandhi, for it granted him the moral and civilizational stature to confront colonial rule. It allowed him to remain engaged in a dialogue with those (representing the majority of the population) who did not wish to renounce their religion in favour of modern secular worldviews. More important, his faith granted him the resolve to define politics and ethics, also politics and religion, in mutually intelligible terms:

> No Indian who aspires to follow the way of true religion can afford to remain aloof from politics. In other words, one who aspires to a truly religious life cannot fail to undertake service as his mission, and we are today so much caught up in the political machine that service of the people is impossible without taking part in politics....
>
> The ideal of service implied that one accept sacrifice and suffering as natural and penance and atonement as necessary: "A *sanyaasi* [renouncer] is one who cares for others. He has renounced all selfishness. But he is full of sleepless and selfless activity."[4]

Gandhi's Hinduism was a vastly inventive one. He not only redefined its tenets but also endowed it with a discursive identity that reflected his own experience of it. He deftly detached evil social and cultural practices, as well as religious principles that justified them, from the crucial Hindu "core" that he reconstructed. His marvellous rhetoric of faith, experience and ethics subsumed the structural contradictions that underwrote Hinduism in its everyday social and cultural existence.

This curious yoking of the political and the moral within the matrix of religion allowed Gandhi and his followers to hold politically problematic positions while remaining morally incorruptible and scrupulously spiritual. As far as untouchability was concerned, Gandhi did not favour civic action as much as he did individual soul-searching and spiritual reflection. His emphasis on personal transformation and on the integrity of the individual conscience possessed a sharp dramatic edge that could hold captive the public imagination, as we shall see in what follows.

Political rights and human dignity

In 1930 the British government convened a round-table conference to discuss with Indians the future of governance and the framing of a constitution for India. Dr Babasaheb Ambedkar, the great anti-caste ideologue and Dalit leader, submitted a memorandum to the conference, outlining a set of demands. Among other things his memorandum drew attention to the political rights of the untouchables:

The depressed classes must be given sufficient political power to influence legislative and executive action for the purpose of securing their welfare. In view of this they demand that the following provisions shall be made in the electoral law so as to give them:

1) right to adequate representation in the Legislatures of the Country, Provincial and Central;
2) right to elect their own men as representatives by adult suffrage, and by separate electorates for the first ten years and thereafter joint electorates and reserved seats. (47)

Gandhi vehemently opposed this demand for separate electorates. Claiming that he wished to save the untouchables from themselves, he argued:

If they had separate electorates, their lives would be miserable in villages which are the stronghold of Hindu orthodoxy. It is the superior class of Hindus who have to do penance for having neglected the untouchables for ages. That penance can be done by active social reform and making the lot of the untouchables more bearable by acts of service but not by asking for separate electorates for them. By giving them separate electorates, you will throw the apple of discord between the untouchables and the orthodox. (70)

Ambedkar pointed out that Gandhi's emotive response to untouchability denied political subjectivity and agency to the untouchables and made them eternally dependent on the goodwill and troubled conscience of upper-caste Hindus.

To ask the Hindus to undertake the removal of untouchability is good advice. But to go to the length of assuring oneself that the Hindus are so overwhelmed with a sense of shame for the inhuman treatment they have accorded to the untouchables that they dare not fail to abolish untouchability and that there is band of Hindu reformers pledged to do nothing but remove untouchability is to conjure an illusion to fool the untouchables and to fool the world at large. (39)

This indictment, however, did not deter Gandhi. He defended himself on moral grounds. As a Hindu, he had to atone for the sins of his forefathers, and one vital part of this process of atonement required him to love and hold the untouchables in reverence. They were *harijans*, betrayed children of a good God. He and other contrite Hindus like him must pay for that betrayal. Since upper-caste Hindus were responsible for the existence of untouchability, they ought to abolish it: "Neither struggles by Dalits, nor state policies in their favour were as morally acceptable to Gandhi as the individual choices exercised by remorseful upper-caste Hindus. For this would imply that upper-caste Hindus had become so unregenerate that they had to be pressured into action. Further he firmly believed that 'Man cannot be made good by Law'."[5]

To preserve his moral arguments and act on his offended moral sensibility, Gandhi undertook a fast, proclaiming that the granting of separate electorates to the untouchables would divide Hindu society into two irreconcilable sections.

"I hold that separate electorate is harmful for [the depressed classes] and for Hinduism, whatever it may be from the purely political standpoint.... So far as Hinduism is concerned, separate electorates would simply vivisect and disrupt it.

"For me the question of these classes is predominantly moral and religious. The political aspect, important though it is, dwindles into insignificance compared to the moral and religious issue....

"I have been interested in the condition of these classes from my boyhood and have more than once staked my all for their sake. I say this not to pride myself in any way. For I feel that no penance that the Hindus may do can in any way compensate for the calculated degradation to which they have consigned the depressed classes.

"But I know that separate electorates is neither a penance nor any remedy for the crushing degradation.... I therefore respectfully inform His Majesty's Government that in the event of their decision creating separate electorate for the depressed classes, I must fast unto death."

Gandhi's passionate espousal of the cause of untouchables was as much due to his strong sense of himself as a Hindu, as it was to his revulsion against the practice of untouchability. (78)

The fast proved to be an epic one. It pushed the Hindu upper castes into hurriedly opening the doors of their homes and temples to untouchables. Thousands of Hindu men and women queued up to receive food from the hands of untouchables. Ambedkar, however, was not moved by these gestures. He plainly told Gandhi that the Mahatma had been unfair to him and his people. Protracted negotiations followed, with Ambedkar holding on to his position that the untouchables deserved their political safeguards. Gandhi refused to accept the validity of separate electorates and reiterated his earlier argument that it would divide the Hindu community permanently and pitch the untouchables into the dark heartland of upper-caste hatred.

Finally, Gandhi and Ambedkar agreed that untouchables would be granted reserved seats in electoral constituencies. This arrangement would guarantee them a representative from the community, while keeping them united with the upper-caste voters. Ambedkar had saved Gandhi's life, knowing full well that if anything happened to the Mahatma, the untouchables would have to pay dearly for it. Gandhi relished his martyred moment. True to his belief that "joy comes out of pain, voluntarily borne", he had prepared himself for what he believed to be his final act of penitence.

Gandhi's position on untouchability demonstrates both the possibilities and the limits of a politics that looks to an ethics of reconciliation for a resolution of its concerns. Though Gandhi did not directly work with notions of forgiveness and reconciliation, he did insist that the issue of untouchable dignity and freedom could not be viewed solely in terms of the material and social contradictions that defined their relationship with upper-caste Hindus. Rather, untouchables had to be viewed as necessary and valued constituents of the larger Hindu community. In this sense, he did subscribe to a politics of reconciliation, without actually situating his efforts and ideas within an ethical problematic that derived from notions of sin, penitence and forgiveness.

Relationship between politics and ethics

Gandhi's ideas were subjected to an exhaustive criticism both during his lifetime and thereafter. Ambedkar's criticisms of Gandhi were fundamental and profound, expounding a radically different relationship between politics and ethics. While agreeing with Gandhi that untouchability was morally repugnant, Ambedkar insisted that its essential horror ought not to distract attention from the premises that sustain it: an economics that is pitiless and a civics that is cynical.

> Most people believe that untouchability is a religious system. This is true. But it is a mistake to suppose that it is only a religious system.... It is also an economic system which is worse than slavery.... As an economic system it permits exploitation without obligation. Untouchability is not only an economic system of unmitigated exploitation but it is also a system of uncontrolled economic exploitation. (197)

The economics of untouchability had made it impossible (and unprofitable) for Hindus to develop a moral sense.

> History, I am afraid, will not justify the conclusion that a Hindu has a quick conscience or if he has it is so active as to charge him with moral indignation and drive him to undertake a crusade to eradicate the wrong. History shows that where ethics and economics come into conflict, victory is always with economics. Vested interests have never been known to have willingly divested themselves unless there was sufficient force to compel them. (197)

Given that the moral sense of the Hindus was suspect, the ineffable inner voice of conscience, so dear to Gandhi, cannot be relied upon to abolish untouchability. Untouchables, argued Ambedkar, needed acts, not words and noble gestures of faith. Direct action required that the untouchables be actively assisted in the securing of their civic rights, even if this meant "prosecuting Hindus who assault untouchables or proclaim social and economic boycott against them and thereby prevent them from exercising their rights" (253). In the memorandum he submitted to the round-table conference, Ambedkar outlined concrete proposals that would realize such prosecutions under the law. He also insisted that the state had a role to play in adjudicating matters that involved crimes against untouchables – it must invest untouchables with rights and must endeavour to protect them. He categorically stated that "the forces of Law and Order must be on our side, if it is to end in success" (136).

Unlike Gandhi, Ambedkar favoured state intervention in civil, cultural and religious life. He was not convinced that upper-caste Hindus would suffer a change of heart, and besides, even if they did, their sensibilities could not be made the measure of reform. Such changes were, of necessity, arbitrary and mercurial, governed by the emotions of the hour, dictated by contingencies such as Gandhi's epic fast. Ambedkar preferred to rely on the iron guarantees that a strong state could assure rather than on civic goodwill. He observed: "India wants a dictator like Kemal Pasha or Mussolini in social and religious matters."[6]

Ambedkar's insistence on direct action was also a tangential response to the grand drama of fasting, penance, meditation and soul-searching that Gandhi advocated. Gandhi's piety in this respect was not an empty one, but more often than not, it merely made a gesture towards change, rather than actually effecting it. In an exhaustive critique of the actual projects undertaken by Gandhi's followers for the amelioration of the untouchables, Ambedkar pointed to the various sins of omission and half-heartedness that had dogged the realization of their objectives. He was clear on this matter: Gandhi's good intentions, his suffering conscience, his remonstrance to upper-caste Hindus were all very well, but they had not resulted in concrete changes in the lives of untouchables. They had simply given political and ethical currency to an ideology that, at best, was ambiguous and, at worse, dubious (103-45).

Where Gandhi counselled his followers to "assume" the demeanour of an untouchable, Ambedkar argued that the deep sense of difference and alienation that divided Hindu society into touchables and untouchables required something more difficult and less dramatic. He pointed out that all relationships in caste society are mechanical and opportunistic.

> The caste in India is exclusive and isolated. There is no interaction and no modification of aims and objects. What a caste or a combination of castes regard as their "own interest" as against other castes remains as sacred and inviolate as ever. The fact that they mingle and cooperate does not alter their character. These acts of cooperation are mechanical and not social. Individuals use one another so as to get desired results without reference to the emo-

tional and intellectual disposition. The fact that they give and take orders modifies actions and results. But it does not affect their disposition. [It] could be overcome only through concrete acts of mutuality. (193)

In such a society, no spectacular change of heart is possible. Rather than "become" untouchables to experience remorse and practise penitence, upper-caste Hindus would do well to give up their exclusivity and discover the virtues of mutuality. This was a worthwhile ideal in place of what he termed Gandhian charity, which, he argued, sought to kill the untouchable with its kindness. Charity towards the untouchables invariably denied them ethical and political agency, whereas an ideal of mutuality that drew them into a wider social arc opened up possibilities of commingling and communication. Arguing that campaigns against untouchability must involve untouchables as social workers and campaigners, he noted: "As Tolstoy said, 'Only those who love can serve'.... I do not suggest that there are not scoundrels amongst the depressed classes who have not made social service their last refuge. But largely speaking you can be sure that a worker drawn from the depressed classes will regard the work as love's labour..." (139)

If untouchables were to be autonomous agents, subjects of their history and masters of their destiny, the solution lay not in elevating their dreary labour to the status of a penance, as Gandhi sought to do, but in educating them and providing them with equal employment opportunities. This latter position was especially important, since untouchables were barred from several professions for fear that they might "defile" them. For Ambedkar, the ideals of mutuality and autonomy were, clearly, inseparable and existed in a reciprocal relationship. Mutuality represented a plea for an associated life, a shared social existence, whereas autonomy was the premise upon which an associated life could be built. Autonomy, in this instance, implied not merely an economic and political empowerment of the untouchables but an ontological imperative. It implied an acknowledgment of the untouchable's bodily and mental integrity – in essence, his or her very being.

A religion of social equality

Ambedkar's final argument with Gandhi on the subject of untouchability was his most radical as well. As we have seen, Gandhi's obsessive concern with the cause of untouchables was informed by a sensibility that defined itself as "Hindu". Ambedkar took issue with Gandhi's insistence that untouchables were also Hindus.

Can the untouchable be held to be part of the Hindu society? Is there any human tie that binds them to the rest of the Hindus? There is none. There is no connubium. There is no commensualism. There is not even the right to touch, much less to associate.... The whole tradition of the Hindus is to recognize the untouchable as a separate element and insist upon it as a fact. (138)

These questions were purely rhetorical. Ambedkar knew that neither Hindu reformers nor Gandhi would heed his remonstrance. For one, Gandhi had declared that though he was against untouchability, he was not against the caste system. Besides, as Ambedkar himself argued on other occasions, Hinduism was essentially supportive of caste and the divisions it sanctioned, including the consigning of a vast section of people to menial tasks and to perpetual untouchability. Yet, Ambedkar chose to pose these questions, if only to point out that no reconciliation was possible between upper-caste Hindus and untouchables, unless the upper castes mended their ways. Expressions of remorse were not enough for him and others like him; they had to be demonstrated to be true in and through practical ethical and political acts, mandated by an honest, critical reflection on individual, social and religious sensibilities. If such reflections were not forthcoming, then they would have to be enabled, even coerced, into existence, through legal fiat and the authority of the state.

For Ambedkar, Hinduism did not connote a moral dilemma. He did not think that its civilizational importance was central to definitions of national identity and in the struggle against the British. However, Hinduism interested and troubled him for other reasons. He wanted to probe into its historical and cultural life for the verdicts it pronounced in favour of or against the caste system. He wished to know how and through what means this religion came to favour the division of human society into mutually exclusive communities. He thus undertook systematic investigations of its hierarchies, its vertical and horizontal divisions. In this sense, Hinduism for him was a critical object of knowledge, not a frame of experience. His relationship to it was always critical, rather than affective. His ultimate rejection of Hinduism was also on these grounds – it possessed neither the affective power nor the requisite social and political resources to enable untouchables to participate in civic and national life as valued and equal citizens.

In the mid-1930s he publicly declared that though he was born a Hindu, he would not die as one, implying that he intended to convert to another religion. When he actually did convert to Buddhism in 1956, along with thousands of untouchables, the signals he sent out were unmistakable. Hinduism had failed him and his people, he seemed to say, and if they were not to merely live out their lives in simultaneously indicting Hinduism and coming to terms with it in an everyday sense, they had to demonstrate that they desired to live differently. Clearly, if the past could not be healed, then it had to be remembered differently. What could not be reconciled must be situated elsewhere – in other narratives and memories, in other sorts of everyday acts.

Ambedkar's choice of Buddhism as his new religion was not only on account of its catholic humanity and gospel of freedom and peace. He clearly regarded Buddhism as offering radical civic possibilities. As we have seen, he relied on both civic and sacral instruments for effecting change. He demanded that untouchables be granted their civic rights; he insisted on their enforcement, if necessary, through prosecution. Later, through his work in the Constitutional Assembly, he gave life and form to the nation's self-representations. He made sure that the abolition of untouchability was defined as a constitutional right. He also included within the directive principles of the constitution provisions that would mitigate the effects of its vile economics. (Not all his formulations in this respect were accepted by the Constituent Assembly.)

Ambedkar did not rest on his civic achievements. He could never entirely put away his misgivings about the mental dispositions of the Hindu upper castes. His experiences in the Constituent Assembly had demonstrated to him that civic and political freedoms and guarantees could and would be stymied by Hindu upper-caste prejudice and rancour. The spirit of Hinduism, he was convinced, would compromise the content of his radical civics and politics, retard their realization.

He therefore felt the need to take up a religious and ethical worldview that would negotiate creatively with the new civics. Buddhism appeared an appropriate choice because it was a religion that centred on human beings and not God. In the dedication he appended to one of his books (the present vol. 9), he drew attention to the words of Ruth in the Old Testament: "For whither thou goest, I will go; and where thou lodgest, I will lodge; thy people shall be my people, and thy God my God." He commented: "Ruth's statement... defined ancient society by its most dominant characteristic, namely that it was a society of man plus God while modern society is a society of men only (pray remember that in men I include women)." He had long wanted to write on this theme. His encounters with Gandhi finally made him do so. But perhaps there lay hidden between those lines another aspiration: a desire for a religion that did not have to heed God.

Ambedkar's critique of Gandhi and his conversion to Buddhism enable us fix critical limits to a politics of reconciliation. Sensitive to the immense charisma that emanated from Gandhi and conscious of Gandhi's power to enthral and convince people through dramatic and spectacular public acts (fasting, non-violent resistance to violence, defying government through highly visible acts of civil disobedience), Ambedkar resolved to discover the material underside to the Mahatma's mystique. In doing so, he came to define new and radical notions of reconciliation, arguing for an ethics that would achieve fruition in a transformed social order. To effect that transformation, he outlined a new civics and politics, animated and enlivened by the religion of the Buddha.

NOTES

[1] Neville Alexander, "Dealing with the Past: Truth and Reconciliation in South Africa", paper presented at a conference "'Wahrheit' und 'Versöhnung' in Südafrika", held at KruppVorlesungen zu Politik und Geschichte, Oct. 1999. All quotations regarding the TRC are taken from this paper.

[2] In contemporary India, the so-called untouchables are commonly referred to as, and prefer to be known as, Dalits. (The word "dalit" is from Marathi, a western-Indian language, and means "oppressed".) Gandhi favoured the term "harijans", while in government and public parlance, the so-called untouchables were referred to as the depressed classes. Ambedkar uses the latter term. I have used all terms, allowing the context to dictate usage.

[3] Gandhi, in *Young India,* 20 Oct. 1920, quoted in Babasaheb Ambedkar, *Writings and Speeches,* vol. 9, *What Congress and Gandhi Have Done to the Untouchables,* Bombay, Thacker, 1945, p.38. Subsequent page numbers in the text refer to this volume.

[4] Quoted in Bhikhu Parekh, *Colonialism, Tradition and Reform: An Analysis of Gandhi's Political Discourse,* New Delhi, Sage, 1989, pp.92,94.

[5] *Ibid.,* p.232.

[6] Quoted in Rajmohan Gandhi, *The Good Boatman: A Portrait of Gandhi,* New Delhi, Viking, 1995, p.259.

Contributors

Tissa Balasuriya OMI is director of the Centre for Religion and Society, Colombo, Sri Lanka.

Marlene Cuthbert is professor emeritus at the University of Windsor, Ontario, Canada.

William F. Fore is former head of the communication commission of the National Council of Churches in the USA, and former president of the World Association for Christian Communication.

Bernie Harder is associate professor in the English department, University of Windsor, Ontario, Canada.

Nawaf Kabbara is president of the Arab Organization of Disabled People, Beirut, Lebanon.

Jahda Abou Khalil is general director of the Arab Organization of Disabled People, Beirut, Lebanon.

Epp Lauk is associate professor of journalism at the University of Tatu, Estonia.

Dafne Sabanes Plou from Argentina is a free-lance journalist specializing in church and society issues.

Carlos A. Valle is general secretary of the World Association for Christian Communication, London, UK.